Village W
— in —
NORTH YORKSHIRE

Village Walks
in
NORTH YORKSHIRE

Len Markham

COUNTRYSIDE BOOKS
NEWBURY, BERKSHIRE

First published 1997
© Len Markham 1997

COUNTRYSIDE BOOKS
3 Catherine Road
Newbury, Berkshire

ISBN 1 85306 488 2

Front cover photograph of Gayle in
Upper Wensleydale taken by
Bill Meadows

Designed by Graham Whiteman
Photographs by the author
Maps by Christine Markham

Produced through MRM Associates Ltd., Reading
Printed by Woolnough Bookbinding Ltd., Irthlingborough

Contents

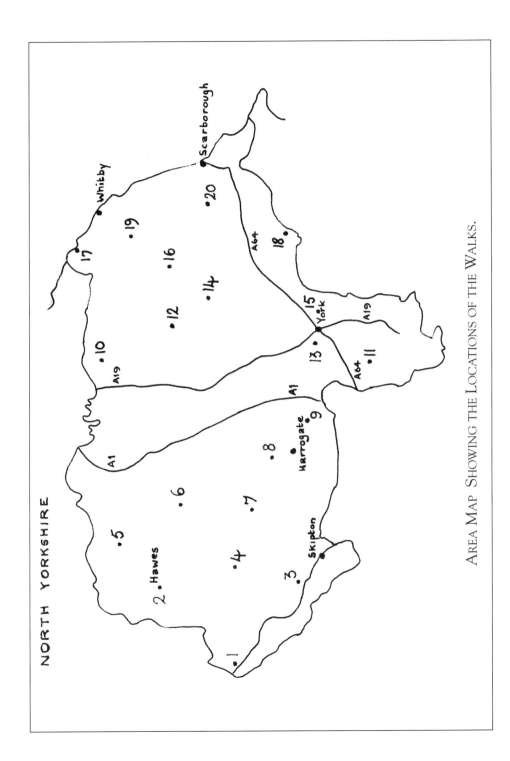

AREA MAP SHOWING THE LOCATIONS OF THE WALKS.

ॐ

Publisher's Note

We hope that you obtain considerable enjoyment from this book; great care has been taken in its preparation. Although at the time of publication all routes followed public rights of way or permitted paths, diversion orders can be made and permissions withdrawn.

We cannot of course be held responsible for such diversion orders and any inaccuracies in the text which result from these or any other changes to the routes nor any damage which might result from walkers trespassing on private property. We are anxious though that all details covering the walks are kept up to date and would therefore welcome information from readers which would be relevant to future editions.

Introduction

The third of the fabled Ridings, North Yorkshire is a county of immense space and geographical variety that has largely avoided the industrialisation of neighbouring areas. Green and unspoilt, it is famous for its moors and dales, a heritage of drystone walls and ancient field boundaries, historic houses and abbeys, and a treasure trove of more modern attractions. It beckons to be explored on foot, and what better way than through its villages, joined as they are by a solid network of both long and short distance footpaths. And not just footpaths – there are Roman roads, drovers' trails, smugglers' tracks and lost railway lines. All have been walked in devising what I believe you will find a wonderful walking experience.

The purpose of this book has been to select 20 of the best North Yorkshire villages and their surroundings, visiting period homes, churches, castles, monastic ruins, monuments, village greens, ponds and entwining rural footpaths and byways, linked to create the very best country walks. Some short and untaxing, some a little longer, each walk is circular and is accompanied by details of those other essential village institutions - teashops and inns. There is also supplementary information about visitor centres and local produce and craft shops.

None of the walks ventures too far from civilisation, although mud and other organic matters are likely to be encountered even on the sunniest days and stout shoes and waterproofs are recommended. Each walk is allied to a sketch map, designed to guide you to the starting point and give a simple but accurate idea of the route to be taken. However, for those who like the benefit of detailed maps, the Ordnance Survey Landranger 1:50 000 series – and the excellent Outdoor Leisure 1:25 000 sheets, where available – are very much recommended, particularly for identifying the main features of views. The relevant map numbers are therefore included.

This, my eighth Yorkshire walking book, has been even more of a delight to research and compile than all the others. In all weathers and in all seasons I have enjoyed every stride. I hope you will follow in my footsteps soon.

Len Markham

INGLETON

Length: 6 miles

Getting there: Ingleton is on the A65 Skipton to Kendal road between Settle and Kirkby Lonsdale.	**Parking:** Park in the Community Centre pay and display car park.	**Maps:** OS Landranger – Wensleydale and Upper Wharfedale (98) and Outdoor Leisure – Yorkshire Dales Western (2) (GR 694729).

Limestone and water have made Ingleton famous, the generous rainfall of centuries having percolated and poured to sculpt caves, potholes and waterfalls. Until 1885 the series of dramatic falls on the river Twiss were inaccessible to the general public. Now the visitors come in droves to enjoy the torrents and the wild mountain scenery. In the village, where every manner of walking apparel can be bought, the Twiss combines with the river Doe to form the salmon honoured Greta. Ingleton is a centre for walking pilgrimages to the great triumvirate of Ingleborough, Whernside and Penygent. The 26 mile round trip to the three summits must be completed

A waterfall at Ingleton.

FOOD and DRINK

There are six or more cafés and tearooms in the village offering everything from cream teas to oriental cuisine. The Curlew Craft Centre near the viaduct is recommended for vegetarian meals. The Three Horseshoes inn is open all day, its menu featuring Cumberland sausage in 7 inch Yorkshire puddings and a selection of steaks. Telephone: 01524 241247.

within 12 hours to qualify for Yorkshire citizenship.

As a boy I used to collect the names of steam engines. Fifty years on, I have an appetite for Yorkshire dales. Lonely Kingsdale is my 127th. What an acquisition! Stepping the limestone fantastic with uninterrupted views of Ingleborough, this taxing but invigorating hike takes us, incredibly, to scenery unchanged in 12,000 years. Glaciated escarpments of contorted and fractured rock, potholes and limestone pavements with their characteristic clints and grykes dominate the higher parts of the dale, the lower footpaths returning us to Ingleton via the cataracts and falls. Sturdy boots and a sure foot will be needed for this splendid walk.

THE WALK

❶ From the car park, turn right on the road under the viaduct and go next left downhill. At the bottom, go left again, following the signs to the waterfalls. Cross the bridge and by the entrance to the waterfalls, go right, following the footpath sign to Thornton Hall. Go through the kissing-gate and keep wallside to the second kissing-gate. Keep forward following the yellow arrow marker, going round the barn and keeping wallside to the corner. Cross the stile, heading up and across the meadow, aiming for the top end of the lower barn. Mount the steps and go right following the public footpath sign to the farmstead. Go left through the double gates of the stock pen to the road.

❷ Turn right on the road and go uphill for 150 yards, then turn left, following the footpath signed to Westgate Lane. Go through the gate and veer right across the meadow to a stile in the top corner. Cross and head for the empty Cowgill Farm, crossing the meadow to the farmyard. Go over the ladder stile and walk on between the buildings (preserved privy on the left), going right, heading for the topside of the field. Go through the gap in the wall in the corner and keep wallside to the next wall crossing. Go through and keep wallside to the stile and the road.

❸ Turn right on the road uphill and go next left on the track signposted 'Unsuitable For Motors'. Continue left through two gates to the Masongill Treatment

PLACES of INTEREST

White Scar Cave is 1½ miles from Ingleton on the B6255 Hawes road. An 80 minute tour explores the 200,000 year old cave system on a 1 mile illuminated pathway. Hard hats are provided. Also along the B6255 is the impressive **Ribblehead Viaduct** on the Settle – Carlisle railway. Many of the workers who built this towering structure never lived to tell the tale. A plaque to commemorate the fatalities is in the tiny church of St Leonard at Chapel-le-Dale on the old Roman road 3 miles from Ingleton.

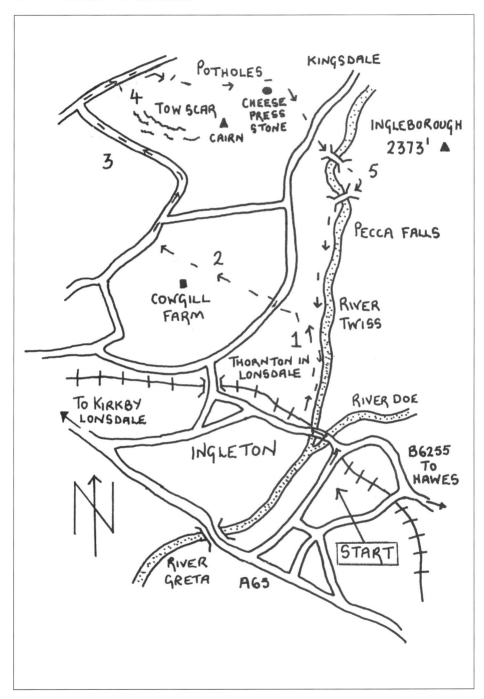

Works. Turn right on the steeply ascending track.

❹ Go through the gate and swing right and left, keeping on wallside for about 300 yards after the wall corner, turning right opposite a solitary tree. The next part of the walk although on a public footpath is ill-defined, weaving its way through the pavements and over loose rock. Steer well left of the cairn on the edge of the scar, heading direct for Ingleborough's summit, and walk towards a second, smaller, more rounded cairn, passing left of the giant square stone known as the Cheese Press. In this inviolate landscape, you will find rare ferns and flowers in the crevices.

Weave left downwards through the tumble of rocks – a real labyrinth – going right to find a ladder stile. Cross and keep descending on a grassy path to a wall. Cross a ladder stile to the road.

❺ Go left for 50 yards and turn right on a green road, going through a gate to cross a footbridge over the river Twiss. Continue on the ascending track and at the Ingleton Waterfalls Walk sign go right. This wonderful finish to the walk is through private land and a small fee is payable on exiting. Follow the well maintained trail for about 1½ miles back into Ingleton. At the exit, turn left and return to the car park.

HAWES

Length: 6 miles

Getting there: Hawes is in Upper Wensleydale on the A684 west of Aysgarth.	Parking: On-street and pay and display parking is available in the village but it can get busy especially during the summer months.	Maps: OS Outdoor Leisure – Yorkshire Dales Northern and Central (30) and Landranger – Wensleydale and Upper Wharfedale (98) (GR 873898).

I have scores of maps in my bookcase – the old 1 inch Wensleydale (price 6/6d!) is more dog-eared than all the rest. Plumb centre of this archive, still discernible through a patina of muck, sweat and occasional tears, is the 'mother of Wensleydale' – Hawes, a wild west village cum market town squeezed into the valley of the Ure

between high fells. Every road seems to converge on Hawes and walks galore radiate from its busy centre which in every season is alive with visitors.

Taking in the picturesque neighbouring village of Gayle, part of this high fell walk treads Cam High Road, the Roman road between Ilkley and Bainbridge –

Burtersett High Pasture, with the Cam High Road disappearing into the distance.

'Keep it straight Claudius, our chariots can't turn corners'. There are panoramic views all round from the skirt of Wether Fell.

THE WALK

❶ Walk up to the parish church of St Margaret and go through the entrance gate towards the door. Turn right and go left through a side gate onto a path. Go through a gap in the wall and swing right on the Pennine Way, on the flagged pathway, following the public footpath sign. Go through the wicket gate and turn left into Gayle.

❷ Go left over the bridge (the cascades above are a favourite subject for painters) and fork left on the Bainbridge road for 50 yards. Turn right through a gap in a wall, following the footpath marked to Burtersett and Marsett. Go through a kissing-gate, steering slightly left across the field, and then go through a wicket gate near the corner. Keep veering left across the next field and go through a gap in a wall, heading for a barn. Pass through another gap and head for a field corner then go right over the ladder stile, following the footpath sign to Burtersett. Take the lower of the two tracks, heading left of the barn, and go through a gap in the wall. Arc left, following the signpost to Burtersett. Go through the gap by the fence and then through the gap in the wall by the top barn, crossing the field to a gap in another wall. Go through and cross a field, going through a gap in the wall by the gate and continuing to the right of the next barn. Continue on Shaws Lane into the village of Burtersett. Swing right in the centre of the village and take the footpath by the barn, signposted to Marsett.

❸ Go through a gap in the wall and through a wicket gate following the yellow arrow marker uphill, heading for the left-hand corner of the wood. Go through a gap in a wall left across a field and then through two further wall gaps, veering away left of the wood. Go through a gap in a wall and continue the ascent, passing an ancient chalybeate spring – High Rigg Well – on the way to the summit. Go through the next gap in the wall, keeping forward on the broad track. Walk through the wicket gate and the gap in the wall, onto Cam High Road.

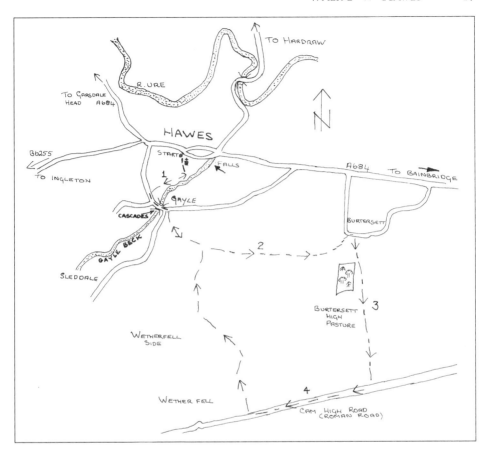

❹ Turn right on the ascending track for 900 yards and go right following the footpath sign to Gayle. Go through the wicket gate and follow the narrow path, swinging left and right through a gateway (there is a hut with a rusted corrugated roof to the left). Go left through a gap in a wall with the shoulder of the fell to the left and drop down through the tussocky grass to cross a broken wall. Drop down right wallside, heading for a clump of trees. Go through a gap in a wall, arcing off left of the trees. Drop down left over a stream and go immediately right through a gap in the wall at the side of the gully. Drop down left, heading for the church. At the signpost keep heading forward and go through a gap in the wall, swinging right. Pass through a gap in another wall, cross a field and go through a wicket gate, forking left and arcing right to a gap in a wall. Go through, turning left, back on the outward route to Gayle and Hawes.

AIRTON

Length: 3½ miles

Getting there: Airton is north-west of Gargrave and Skipton off the A65 road. Go due north from Coniston Cold through Bell Busk.	Parking: Park around the village green. Alternative verge parking may be available east of the village over the Aire bridge.	Maps: OS Landranger - Blackburn and Burnley (103) and Outdoor Leisure - Yorkshire Dales Southern (10) (GR 902594).

Airton is a handsomely preserved and cheery former mill village beside the Aire, its dapperness reflecting the joy of the infant river, a bright and boisterous stream that figures in the annals of a certain chimney sweep called Tom. I quote from *The Water Babies* by Charles Kingsley. '. . . he was not a bit surprised, and went on to the bank of the brook, and lay down on the grass, and looked into the clear, clear, limestone water, with every pebble at the bottom bright and clean, while the little silver trout dashed about in fright at his black face; and he dipped his hand in and found it so cool, cool, cool; and he said, "I will be a fish; I will swim in the

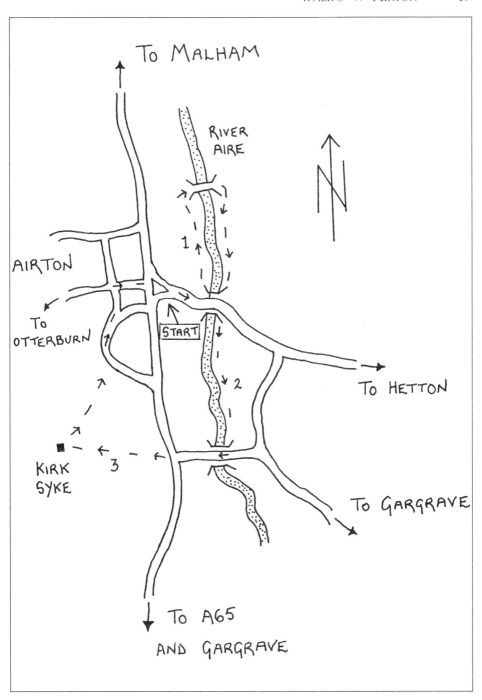

The infant Aire.

water; I must be clean, I must be clean.'" From the triangular green, a delightful lane leads – past a Friends Meeting House of 1700 and the residentially converted old mill – to the river.

On parts of the Pennine Way, we go in search of young Tom along that still scintillating stream. 'Ah, now comes the most wonderful part of this story. Tom, when he woke . . . found himself swimming about in the stream, being four inches, or – that I may be accurate – 3.87902 inches long . . . In fact, the fairies had turned him into a water baby.'

THE WALK

❶ Turn right, down and along the village green passing the Friends Meeting House (round the back is a little cemetery) and go left before the Aire bridge on Riverside Walk over the private car park, passing the converted mill. Walk up the steps, following the footpath sign, and pass the old goit. Cross the bridge near the abandoned sluices and go over the flagged bridge. Cross another bridge and go left over a fourth bridge, swinging right to a kissing-gate. Go through and cross a meadow, then go through a gap in the wall, contin-

uing over the grassland and swinging right to a footbridge over the Aire. Cross to the opposite bank, go through the wicket gate and keep straight forward across the bottom of the meadow. Cross a bridge and go through a gap in a wall, veering right to the abandoned pump house. Continue streamside to the road bridge.

❷ Cross the wall stile and the road and follow the Pennine Way sign down the steps, continuing the walk along the river bank. Go left across the meadow and cross a ladder stile, bearing right to the next stile. Cross this and walk towards the two distinctive trees, then go over a further two stiles. Veer left to the bridge, going up the steps to the gate. Go through and turn right over the bridge.

❸ Keep going forward on the road to the T-junction. Go left on the Bell Busk road for 50 yards and turn right, following the public footpath sign to Kirk Syke through a gate. Continue to a second gate and keep forward, heading between the farm buildings to a stile. Cross and turn right on a track. Swing left at the junction. At the next junction, turn right – notice the old pump – back into the village.

ARNCLIFFE

Length: 7 miles

| Getting there: Arncliffe is in Littondale, north-west of Grassington, off the B6160. | Parking: Park around the village green.

Maps: OS Outdoor Leisure – Yorkshire Dales - Northern and Central and Southern areas | (30 and 10) and Landranger – Wensleydale and Upper Wharfedale (98) (GR 933719). |

On its closely contoured map, Littondale snakes out like a vein of gold compressed by towering scars and crags. Halfway along its 8 mile length is the aptly named conservation village of Arncliffe – 'Eagle's Rock' – a collection of listed farmhouses and cottages surrounding a noble green.

Girded by the Cowside Beck and the incomparably beautiful river Skirfare, Arncliffe was the home of Charles Kingsley (see also the Airton walk) who wrote *The Water Babies* and it has been the setting in more recent years for episodes of the TV series *Emmerdale* . South of the vil-

FOOD and DRINK

The atmospheric Falcon inn on the village green is open for drinks only. The Raikes Cottage Tearoom (over the Cowside Beck bridge and left) offers home-made soups and light lunches. In Kettlewell, the Cottage Tearoom has an extensive menu which includes giant Yorkshire puddings, ham and eggs and cream teas. Telephone: 01756 760405.

lage is Blue Scar where traces of an Iron Age settlement have been found. The surrounding heights are riddled with shake holes, caves and abandoned shafts.

All the delights of hot-air ballooning without ever leaving the ground! This energetic, blowy Arncliffe – Kettlewell – Starbotton classic over Old Cote Moor, along thousand year old tracks, involves the breathless negotiation of stunning moorland. The path is very steep in places and the weather at the summit can be unpredictable, even in summer – so go well prepared.

THE WALK

❶ Head towards the church and the river and cross the bridge, turning right through a gap in a wall and going through a wicket gate, following the footpath sign to Kettlewell. Walk alongside the river, whose bankside church of St Oswald displays a plaque listing names of local men who fought at Flodden Field. Swing left up the steps to the wicket gate, cross the lane and go through another wicket gate, following a 'FP Kettlewell' sign right. Cross a ladder stile over a wall and keep heading right

A bird's eye view of the Wharfe between Starbotton and Kettlewell.

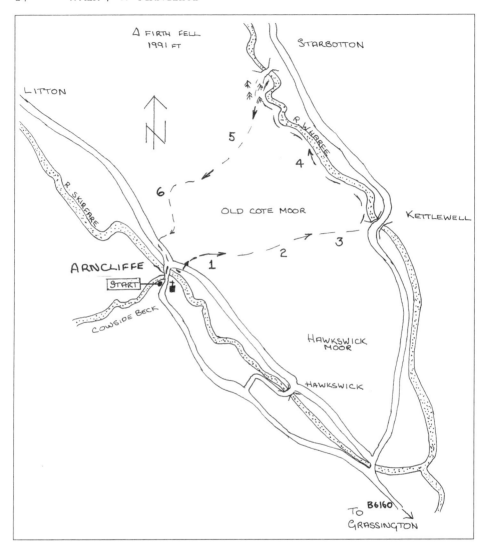

uphill through woodland. Go through a gate and leave the wood on a craggy path, taking a ladder stile over a wall.

❷ Veer off to the right over the moorland. Cross a ladder stile and keep heading right, taking the distinctive path through the heather. Continue up to the footpath

sign. Keep heading generally right to the next footpath sign and bear left across the heather, going right across a ladder stile. Keep going right to the next stile. Cross and still keep right as you drop down.

❸ Ignore the farm track to the right and keep forward along the footpath over the tussocky grass, following the wall down. Climb the ladder stile to the right and swing left, heading towards Kettlewell. Cross the ladder stile and go through the gate left, crossing the bridge into Kettlewell. A busy place, attracting walkers, cyclists and motorists, this village once had 13 pubs!

❹ Leaving Kettlewell, go back over the bridge and turn right through the gate into the National Trust land, following the public footpath sign to Buckden and Starbotton. Follow the well defined riverside path for 1¾ miles along the river Wharfe to the Starbotton bridge.

❺ Turn left along the footpath signposted to Arncliffe. Go left of the barn and through a gate into the woods on a very steep track. Pass through a gate and continue as the track levels out. Go right through a gate, following the footpath sign to Arncliffe. Walk through a gap in the wall and keep going forward, dropping down. Directly opposite on the horizon is the dramatic valley of the Cowside Beck flanked by Yew Cogar Scar and West Moor.

❻ Drop down following the well worn path, passing the shooting lodge (built in 1903) and the bell pits and go through a gate to the road. Turn left back into Arncliffe.

WALK 5

LANGTHWAITE
Length: 5½ miles

Getting there: From Richmond go west on the A6108 and the B6270 to Reeth, then go north-west on the minor road into Arkengarthdale. An alternative, and a very fast and convenient route is to leave the A66 on the minor road south of Barnard

Castle (between Greta Bridge and Bowes), driving over the spectacular Stang.

Parking: You can park on the verge opposite the CB inn. Patrons may use the inn car park – but please ask

before leaving your car while you walk.

Maps: OS Landranger – Barnard Castle (92) and Outdoor Leisure – Northern and Central (30) (GR 999031).

In medieval times, Arkengarthdale was a hunting forest inhabited by boar, deer and wolves. Raped of its timber and lead over 700 years, wild, and in places forbidding, the area has a shivering beauty, a concert of yawning landscapes and skies inducing

an instant lassitude, the release of city tensions having the impact of a burst clock spring. Much of the terrain is pockmarked with old mine workings and spoil heaps. Mellowing now after a century of disuse, these vestiges of an industry that once

FOOD and DRINK

The recently modernised and inviting CB inn has an appealing and cosmopolitan menu, all food being freshly prepared. The eclectic list typically includes pea and ham soup, liver and orange pâté, prawn and cheese fritters, steak and mushroom pie, fillet of pork with orange and spinach and ricotta pancakes. The inn arranges orienteering skill weekends. Telephone: 01748 884567.

Rarely have I fallen asleep whilst exercising a pair of walking boots. With almost 200 different walks to my credit, this has to be the most relaxing. The route takes us through Langthwaite and up, through the incomparably named hamlet of Booze, to the valley of the Slei Gill and the old mine workings. The path returns along the banks of the Arkle Beck.

THE WALK

❶ Turn right from the inn on the Tan Hill road for 100 yards and go right, following a bridlepath sign to Scar House Wood through a gap in a wall and a gate. Drop downhill, arcing right to a gate. Go through and turn right just before the bridge, heading towards the church. Go through the wicket gate to the church.

employed hundreds of men, only add to the mystery of this attractive but little visited part of North Yorkshire. Prominent in Langthwaite are the CB inn (named after a local mine owner), St Mary's church and the Methodist chapel. The generous scale of all three buildings reflects the affluence of lead mining in the 19th century.

St Mary's church.

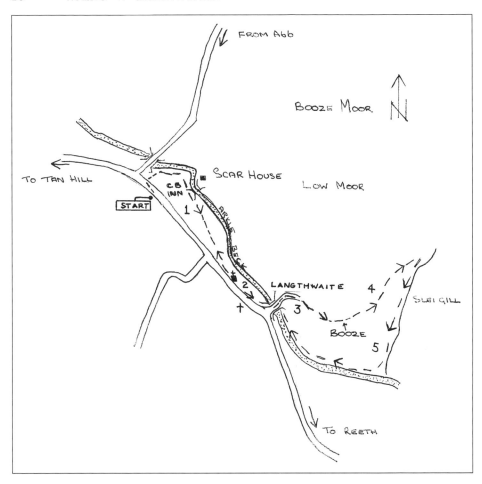

This fairly modern building was erected in 1820, replacing the former 13th-century church at Arkle Town. Its foundations were washed away by a flood.

❷ Continue by the church and merge with the road, going forward on the footway and passing the Wesleyan chapel of 1882. On the right, alongside the green, is a signboard erected by the National Park authorities giving historical information about the lead mining industry.

❸ Go left into Langthwaite over the bridge, following the sign to the Red Lion inn (well worth a visit for a fortifying pint – the route suddenly gets steeper!) and pass through the little circle of cottages, going left on the narrow road uphill. Swing right and follow the road which gradually peters out. Keep following the rough track through Booze, passing several cottages, and swing left, leaving habitation behind.

PLACES of INTEREST

Along the road to the west is the **Tan Hill Inn** – the highest in England at 1,732 ft. The landlord has been known to greet his first New Year's visitors in March! Down the valley is pretty **Reeth**, the largest village in Swaledale. It has an interesting Folk Museum with extensive lead mining displays and a number of attractive shops and restaurants.

❹ Go through a gate and walk on between a wall and a fence, then proceed on a stony track heading up towards a barn and the neck of the valley. Swing left and right by the old workings and pass the barn (once a lead miner's cottage) then gradually drop down for 300 yards on the swardy track towards the gill.

❺ Arc sharp right on the track and gradually drop down on the distinctive path. Cross a stile and go through a gate, keeping straight forward at the direction post. Keep straight forward again at the next direction post, marked to Fremlington and Slei Gill, going through a gate and arcing right on a track. Go through the next gate, entering a wood and continue forward on the beckside path, back into Langthwaite. Turn left and right to retrace your steps to the parking area.

EAST WITTON

Length: 3½ miles

Getting there: East Witton is on the A6108, west of the A1, between Masham and Leyburn.

Parking: Park around the extensive village green.

Maps: OS Landranger – Northallerton and Ripon (99) and Outdoor Leisure – Northern and Central (30) (GR 144860).

The layout of this hill village which occupies a breezy plateau between the heather and the valleys of the Cover and the Ure, reminds me, brought up as I was on cowboy films, of a besieged wagon train, its cottages forming a circle to repel the arrows of the stiff winds that blow in these parts. Surrounding the broadest of village greens, the stone-built dwellings were all

FOOD and DRINK

The Blue Lion provides an adventurous restaurant and bar meal menu lunchtime and evening. Fish dishes are prominent, the range including chargrilled sardines, smoked salmon, roasted monkfish and queen scallops. Typical main course specialities are casseroled wild boar, breast of chicken stuffed with Wensleydale cheese and confit of lamb shoulder. Telephone: 01969 624273.

East Witton church.

largely replaced in 1796 following a disastrous fire. Near the cottages is the characterful Blue Lion inn and, nearby, the church of St John the Evangelist. In the locality are several antiquities, notably a 2 acre hill fort – possibly pre-Roman – and a grotto known locally as Slobbering Sal. East Witton was the site of a stud farm operated by the monks of nearby Jervaulx Abbey.

Wending its way onto the high grouse moor of Witton Fell, this short but exhilarating walk affords the contemplation of a rare wilderness with only the wind and the whirring of wings for company. From the summit a grand panorama unfolds taking in Middleham

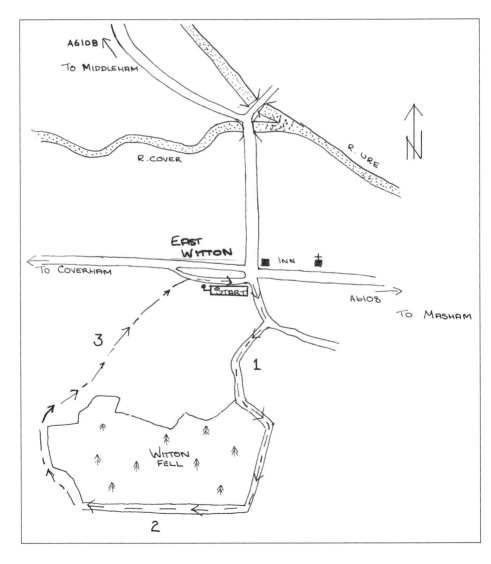

Castle, distant Leyburn and the Cover and Ure, two rivers now blessed by otters.

THE WALK

❶ The walk starts at the bottom of the green by the large glacial boulder. This was brought to the village from a local field by 20 farm horses in 1858. Facing away from the village, turn right on the cul-de-sac road for 150 yards and fork right on the track marked as unsuitable for motor vehicles. Climb steeply uphill, following the winding track, swinging right to the summit.

❷ Ignoring the first right turn, swing second right between the drystone walls to a gate. Go through and continue straight forward, wallside, going through a second gate. Turn right by the end of the wall and drop down, fieldside. Go through a gate and keep wallside to the next gate. Go

PLACES of INTEREST

In the valley bottom are the remains of Jervaulx Abbey, a Cistercian house begun in 1156. Close by at High Jervaulx Farm is the Brymor Ice Cream Parlour. I personally recommend every one of the 30 or so flavours! **Middleham Castle** – the childhood home of the future Richard III is across the valley as is the bustling market town of Leyburn. To the west of the town is **Leyburn Shawl**, a beauty spot forever associated with Mary, Queen of Scots who was apprehended here after escaping from Bolton Castle, some 5 miles distant, in 1568. Her prison cell can still be visited.

through and swing right, dropping down over pasture. Wonderful views unfold from this vantage point.

❸ Go through the red gate and continue downhill, swinging left. Go left through the gate in the bottom and turn right back into the village, making a tour of the village green.

WALK 7

WATH-IN-NIDDERDALE

Length: 5 miles

Getting there: Wath is accessed from Pateley Bridge, reached either on the B6265 Ripon-Skipton road or on the B6165 from Harrogate. Turn first right after leaving Pateley Bridge and proceed for about 2 miles to Wath.

Parking: There is no significant parking in Wath. Park just before the bridge at the side of the bus stop near the river. Alternative parking on busy days is available in Pateley Bridge.

Maps: OS Landranger – Northallerton and Ripon (99) and Outdoor Leisure - Yorkshire Dales Southern (10) (GR 144677).

If Pateley is the soul of Upper Nidderdale, tiny Wath is its sigh. A sequestered hamlet consisting of only a few scattered cottages, a church, a converted railway station and a hotel, its chief attraction, not forgetting the swan-necked bridge, is its delightfully peaceful and leafy setting on the banks of the river. In 1907, walkers, for 3d return from Pateley, could get to Wath by train pulled by such illustrious old engines as *Allenby*, *Kitchener* and *Haig*. The line was opened in September of that year, principally as a mineral railway to serve the construction of Bradford Corporation's Scar House and Angram dams in the high dale. The Nidderdale Light Railway was closed to passenger traffic in December 1929. Part of this walk – some say you can still hear the hiss of steam – follows the abandoned line .

FOOD and DRINK

The Sportsman's Arms Hotel in Wath offers restaurant meals in elegant surroundings. Dishes typically include Nidderdale trout, poached salmon in a dry vermouth and chervil creamy sauce, feuillete of lobster, dales lamb with roasted garlic and breast of ducking with crème de cassis, blackcurrants and oranges. Telephone: 01423 711306. Numerous cafés and restaurants (and a recommended fish and chip shop – see route description) are available in Pateley.

A fine hills and dale, peeps and panoramas saunter combining both hilly tracks and the flat-bottomed paths of the river valley, this ramble visits the busy market town of Pateley Bridge. Enjoy the bustle before melting back into the tranquillity of the Nidd.

THE WALK

❶ From the car park at the side of the bus stop and river in Wath, cross the road and follow the public footpath sign for Heathfield, going through the gap in the wall to the left of the barn. Continue through a gap at the side of the gate and go over a field. Cross a stile, going left uphill and following a yellow arrow marker (aim between the fir trees on the left and a solitary oak on the hillside). Cross a stile, going 15° left, and climb steeply to a second stile. Cross this and walk on, wallside, going left of the cottage. Swing immediately right, following the yellow arrow marker through a gate at the side of the cottage. Continue to a second gate, then turn left on a track to the lane .

❷ Turn right up the lane for 300 yards and go left following the public bridleway and the Nidderdale Way sign for Moss Carr. Swing left on the track and keep following the route signs, going forward,

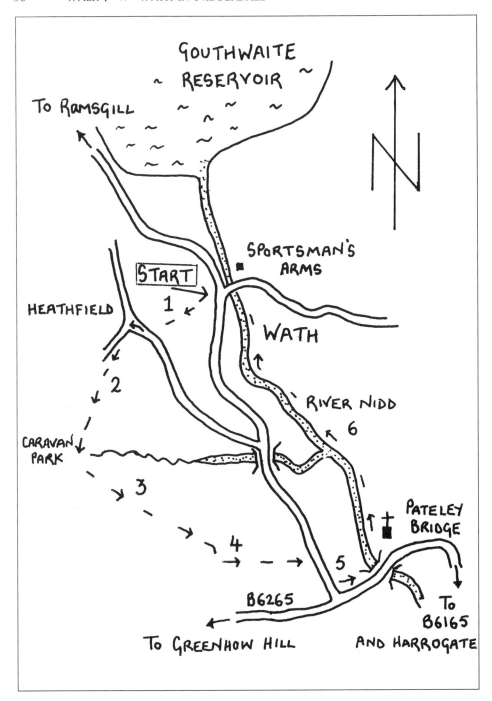

Wath bridge over the river Nidd.

wallside, to a gate. Go through, crossing a field then continuing to the right of a barn and going through another gate. Keeping wallside, follow a blue arrow marker to a further gate. Continue wallside and swing right by the barns, watching out for a blue arrow marker on a post top on the corner of the barn near the farmhouse. Swing left and go straight forward over the farmyard through two gates, dropping down with a stream to the left to a lane. Turn left along the lane.

❸ Walk on for 50 yards and turn right through a gate into a caravan site, following the Nidderdale Way sign over a bridge. Swing right on a track and then left, following the blue arrow marker between

drystone walls. Go left over a footbridge by the cottage, keeping left uphill and following the Nidderdale Way sign. Go through a gate and continue wallside. At the next gate, go through, aiming right, following the yellow arrow marker to a gate. Go through this and keep wallside, following the wall uphill to a gate. Go through and continue to the next gate, from which you access a lane.

❹ Go left on the lane for 150 yards. Just as you enter a fringe of trees, go left following a track. Proceed through a gap in the wall and keep wallside to the kissing-gate in the corner. Go through, keeping wallside, and drop down to a gate. Go through and swing right to the next gate, from which you continue to the road and Pateley Bridge.

❺ Turn right and go left over the bridge into the centre of the town. Thriving Pateley has a number of visitor attractions, not least a wealth of speciality antique and art shops. The Nidderdale Museum opposite the church has a fascinating collection of exhibits depicting dales life and cobbler's shop, general store, Victorian parlour, kitchen, schoolroom, chemist's shop, haberdasher's, joiners's shop and solicitor's office tableaux.

❻ Turn left down King Street (Station Fisheries is here) and go left, following the Nidderdale Way sign. Swing right over the coach park and go left at the fork to the river bank. The walk now follows the route of the former railway. Continue along the well defined track. Two fields before enter-ing Wath, leave the slightly raised remnant of the embankment and go left, crossing the field corner and looking for a gap in the wall just before the trees. Go through, keeping left of the treatment works, and cross a footbridge. Go left over the bridge back to the starting point.

PLACES of INTEREST

Just above Wath is the compensation reservoir of **Gouthwaite** – the mudflats here attract a wide variety of birds. Higher up the valley is **How Stean Gorge** – Yorkshire's Little Switzerland. The spectacular limestone gorge, which is over 80 ft deep in places, is accessed by narrow paths and footbridges. The more adventurous can, torch in hand, visit Tom Taylor's cave. At the top of the valley – access via Water Authority road (parking fee payable) – are the equally impressive **Scar House** and **Angram dams**.

WALK 8

RIPLEY

Length: 3 miles

Getting there: Ripley is signposted to the west of the A61 between Harrogate and Ripon. If approaching from the south, continue through Killinghall, cross the bridge over the Nidd and go left at the next roundabout.

Parking: A large, free, well signposted car park (with toilet facilities) is available on the south side of the village.

Map: OS Landranger – Northallerton and Ripon (99) (GR 284605).

Presenting a fairy tale scene complete with a castle, a historic church, a cobbled square eyed by a petrified beast and a whole main street whisked from a strange sounding land, sublime Ripley is a village in aspic. The serene castle, home of the Ingilby family for over 600 years, is the centrepiece of this delightful estate village where even simple cottages, built with symmetry and orderliness, vie with their imposing neighbour for character. The design of the present village was conceived by Sir William Ingilby after an inspirational tour of Alsace Lorraine in the 1820s, its Gallic notes being echoed in the inscription 'Hotel de Ville' above the old village hall, which, along with almost every other building in Ripley, bears the stone-carved star of grace – the hallmark of its Ingilby origins. A second heraldic element of the Ingilby crest can be found at the southern end of the village near the stocks, a statue of a wild boar commemorating the sterling deeds of Sir Thomas Ingilby, the founder of the dynasty, who in the 14th century, saved Edward III's life by spearing a frenzied animal in the Forest of Knaresborough.

This grand tour of the wider Ingilby estate kicks the dust of six centuries of English history with every stride. Beginning at the village church of All Saints, it visits Ripley's market square and main street, arcing onwards over field and woodland paths. Long distance views over Nidderdale and stately trees are particularly appealing features of this walk which may be linked to an exploration of the extensive castle grounds (entry fee payable).

THE WALK

Leave the car park and walk north, going through the kissing-gate into the village. Enjoy the street scene and the church at leisure before starting the walk proper.

Erected around 1400, the church was re-established on its present site following the loss of the original riverside building to a landslip. In its precincts are a number of attractive tombstones, a unique weeping cross with ensculpted knee niches for pilgrims and, against the chancel wall, gruesome evidence of the execution by firing squad of Royalist soldiers following the battle of Marston Moor in 1644. Inside the church is the exquisite Ingilby Chapel.

FOOD and DRINK

The luxurious Boars Head Hotel overlooking the village square offers quality bar meals and full restaurant facilities, using fresh produce from the Ingilby estate. Telephone 01423 771888. In the courtyard of the castle, Cromwell's Eating House, is popular with families and is ideal for snacks and light meals such as salads, quiches and jacket potatoes. Telephone 01423 772391.

The Weeping Cross in Ripley churchyard.

❶ From the church, turn left and pass the castle entrance, dropping down on Hollybank Lane footpath (Nidderdale Way). Cross the bridge over the outfall from Ripley Castle Lake (fishing available) and walk uphill glancing back for splendid views of the castle. Walk on wallside and at the fork, turn 90° right following the 'Public Footpath Permissive Bridleway' sign towards the barns. Continue on the path wallside, swinging right. Pass the lodge dated 1848 and continue for 50 yards.

❷ Turn left, following the yellow arrow

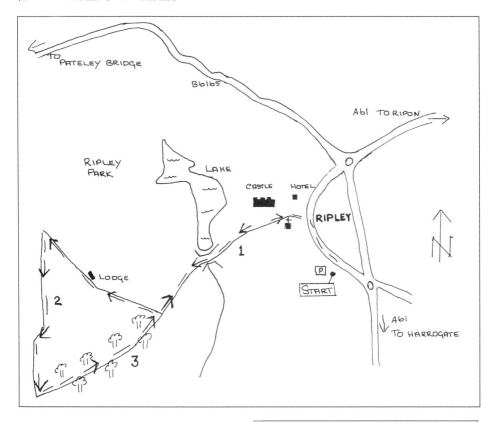

marker on the telegraph pole, going through a kissing-gate and along the edge of a meadow studded with oaks. Walk downhill enjoying the panorama of the Nidd valley. To the right, on the horizon, are the strange sci-fi like radomes of the Menwith Hill Communications Station.

❸ At the field corner, go through a kissing-gate and follow a yellow arrow marker on a descending track passing a cottage on the left. Turn left by the front of the cottage, following a blue arrow marker through a gate uphill into a wood and swing left to rejoin the outward route. Swing right on the track back into Ripley.

PLACES of INTEREST

Ripley Castle and Gardens: Twenty-four generations of Ingilbys have endowed the castle with a rare personality. The homeliest of stately homes, displaying rare furniture and objets d'art alongside photographs of the current Sir Thomas and his family and portraits of many of their illustrious ancestors, the castle is open to the public for intimate conducted tours. Children will be especially captivated by the Knights Chamber with its spiral staircase and priest's hole. The entry fee (reduced price for admission to the gardens only) also gives access to the 5 acre walled garden and hothouses, a deer park and woodland walks and a children's play area. The grounds are home to the National Hyacinth Collection. A children's farmyard/museum is open each Sunday. In the Castle courtyard and village are several craft, gift and speciality food shops.

WALK 9

SPOFFORTH

Length: 6 miles

Getting there: Spofforth is between Wetherby and Harrogate on the A661.	**Parking:** Park on Castle Street.	**Map:** OS Landranger – Leeds and Bradford (104) (GR 363512).

With its 14th-century castle and equally venerable church, Spofforth was a place of importance when Harrogate was just a swamp. Despite suffering at the end of the Civil War, the castle remains a substantial ruin, firing the imagination with its dark corners, its polygonal stair turret and traceried windows. Entry is free. Close by is All Saints' church whose list of rectors goes back to 1310.

Two historical figures dominate Spofforth's considerable hall of fame – the aristocratic Henry Percy who built the castle and the plebeian John Metcalfe – Blind Jack of Knaresborough – who constructed roads. The story of this remarkable man who was blinded by smallpox at birth is wilder than fiction. Sightless, he was a guide, an accomplished horseman and musician, a soldier, haulier, smuggler and road surveyor and builder. He died in his 93rd year leaving 114 directly related offspring! His poetically inscribed tombstone is in All Saints' churchyard.

Through the least known park in York-

shire, this perfect picture of a walk mixes pastures by John Constable, with skies by Ashley Jackson and not a person in sight. Amazingly, not one through road intrudes on this 12 square miles of unspoilt countryside perched like some ancient citadel within a crow's flight of Harrogate, Wetherby and Harewood. In a county where almost every inch has been infiltrated by the tourist hordes, this is the Yorkshire equivalent of the Dark Continent . . . don't miss it!

THE WALK

❶ Walk down Castle Street back into the centre of the village. Keep going straight forward past the Castle Inn on High Street and continue for about 300 yards. Turn right on Park Lane and continue along this lane into Spofforth Park – the route gradually narrows and becomes more track-like. Pass Foxheads farmhouse and keep straight forward. At the fork, keep right following the blue arrow marker (on the post top) hedgeside. Swing left and cross the cattle grid, then follow the track right downhill, hedgeside. Continue fenceside towards the wood. Enter the wood through a gate, following the yellow arrow marker and walk on, keeping to the wood edge. Cross the stile at the end of the wood and keep forward, wallside, for 25 yards. Turn sharp left through a gap in the wall and then sharp right, following the wall to its corner. Head 20° right across a field and go through a gap in a wall following the yellow arrow marker right and then left around the field corner. At the end of the field, go right through the gate and immediately left, following

---

FOOD and DRINK

There are five dining options which include three good inns in Spofforth – the Castle, the William IV and the Railway – all offering bar meals. The Castle is the most convenient, providing recommended fare such as salmon pasta bake, steak and mushroom pie, broccoli potato bake, suet pudding and speciality steaks. Telephone: 01937 590200. Halfway round, the route also passes the Shoulder of Mutton and the hard to resist Star and Garter in the delightful Kirkby Overblow. Try the home-made steak and kidney pie, Yorkshire pudding or gammon and eggs. Telephone: 01423 871625.

Spofforth Castle.

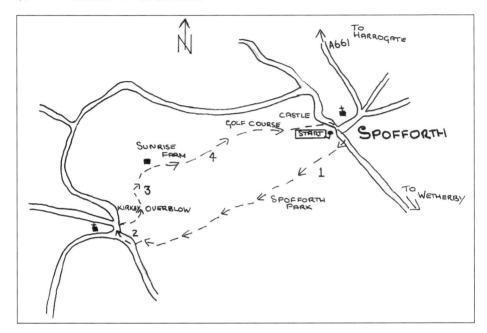

the wall at the back of the houses. Go left over the cattle grid and turn right into Kirkby Overblow.

❷ This hilltop village has wonderful views towards Almscliff Crag. The Garden of Rest in All Saints' churchyard is a fine spot for a picnic. Turn right past the Star and Garter inn and the church. Continue past the Shoulder of Mutton and follow the road as it swings right. At the school road sign, cross the road and go right near Keld Cottage through a gap in a wall, following a public footpath sign.

❸ Keep straight forward, following the wall and a fence, and go left through a gap in the wall by a gate, following the yellow arrow marker. Go through a gate and veer left over a field, dropping down to a bridge over a ditch. Go through the double gates

and follow the arrow marker left uphill to a stile. Cross and walk on, fenceside. Cross the stile in the field corner and go right around the field edge following the yellow arrow marker. Turn left at the corner and halfway up the field switch to the other side of the hedge, keeping straight forward.

PLACES of INTEREST

The internationally famous spa town of **Harrogate** with its upmarket shops, Pump Room Museum and Harlow Carr Botanical Gardens is only 5 miles to the north. **Harewood House,** which is open to the public, is 7 miles south-west. Set in 1,000 acres of parkland, it houses unique treasures including specially made furniture by Chippendale and paintings by El Greco and Titian. It has a renowned tropical bird garden. Just 2 miles north of Spofforth is the lesser known **Plumpton Rocks**, a 23 acre Victorian 'pleasure ground' surrounding a lake.

Go through a gate, following the yellow arrow marker, crossing the field diagonally right to a gate. Go through the gate and veer to the right of Sunrise Farm on a rubble track.

❹ Swing right and continue to the gate. Go through and swing left and right on a track, following the yellow arrow marker. Swing left and go through a gate, then keep straight forward and cross a stile, continuing along a field edge. Follow the hedgeline and drop down on a sunken track to a gate. Go through and cross a stile, swinging right and going left through a gate, following the public bridleway sign.

❺ Follow the wood edge and go through a gate, dropping down left to cross a stream through double gates. Swing right alongside the golf course and go left uphill. Continue on the track, heading for Spofforth church. Drop down and cross a sidestream of the Crimple Beck on a bridge. This watercourse was adopted by the Harrogate based ICI who christened one of their products 'crimplene'. Pass under the old viaduct and swing left back into Spofforth.

CARLTON-IN-CLEVELAND

Length: 6½ miles

Getting there: Due south of Middlesbrough near North Yorkshire's northern boundary, Carlton is just off the A172. The best approach from the south is via the A19 (north of the A1) and then the A172. I can assure motorists coming long distances that the drive is worth it.

Parking: Parking is available immediately opposite the Blackwell Ox inn, across the stream next to the village green. Walkers who intend to patronise the inn can use its car park.

Maps: OS Landranger – Middlesbrough and Darlington (93) and Outdoor Leisure - North York Moors Western (26) (GR 508044).

Any village that cherishes its blacksmith's forge has a soul, and a soul burns brightly in award winning Carlton. Flanking the Alum Beck, which flows from the towering edge of the North York Moors nearby, this red-tiled village has the character of a floral Robin Hood's Bay, the Bristol fashion order and organic symmetry of its distinguished manor house, twin churches and mellow cottages matched by the neatest of village greens and a host of flowers. The village has won the 'Best

FOOD and DRINK

The Blackwell Ox would win rosettes at the Great Yorkshire Show! It specialises in Thai dishes, the oriental menu including tempura king prawns, chicken and sweetcorn soup, mussels with lemon grass and coriander, jumbo spring rolls, stir fried lamb in garlic and soya sauce, spicy Bangkok pork, chicken and ginger and a range of curries. As alternatives, try the home-made steak and ale pie and the duck pie with port and mushrooms. Telephone: 01642 712287.

Kept Village In Forest and Vale' competition and it shows.

The seaside comparison is appropriate for this spirited assault of Little Bonny and Great Bonny Cliffs and the majestic Carlton Bank. From all points of the compass, the bird's-eye views from the summit are tremendous. Part of the route follows the Cleveland Way. An interesting feature of the walk is the abandoned alum mine under Carlton Bank. The profits of this enterprise helped mine owner John Prissick build Carlton's manor house in 1707. This hides coyly, with just a hint of its Queen Anne aloofness, a few yards downstream of the green.

THE WALK

❶ Go up the village street towards Carlton Bank and pass the blacksmith's shop. Can you resist a peep through the door? Turn next right, walking over the footbridge by the ford, and swing right as though going back to the parking area near the green. At the corner of School View Cottage, turn left, following the

The Cleveland Way, near the summit of Carlton Bank – bags of stones (brought in by helicopter) to help with repairs.

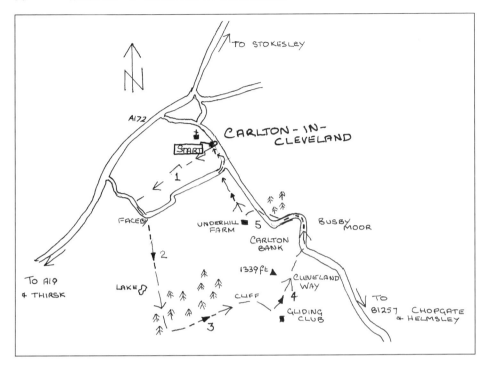

public footpath sign. Proceed for 50 yards and veer left, following the yellow arrow marker over a stile. Continue down the left-hand side of the field to the corner, and cross a footbridge. Swing left and right on the field edge and go through a hedge in the corner, dropping down. Continue on a path between two fields and cross a footbridge in the field corner. Continue down the field hedgeside and keep going forward at the next field. Go through the hedge gap and turn left on the road to Faceby.

❷ Walk uphill and, opposite the Sutton Arms, swing right on the road into Faceby. Keep going forward where the metalled road gives way to a track and proceed gradually uphill, going left and following the blue arrow marker towards the forest.

❸ Continue to the gate and go over the stile, turning immediately right up a bank on a steeply ascending track through the trees. Pass through a wicket gate at the edge of the forest and go left, walking over the spoil heaps and onward on a track through deep bracken. At the fork, take the sunken track to the right, climbing all the while and swinging right, away from the wood. Where the bracken gives way to heather almost near the top, go left on the escarpment path. Middlesbrough can be seen due north. To the north-east is the distinctive conical form of Roseberry Topping.

❹ Walk on along the distinctive path

PLACES of INTEREST

The great explorer Captain James Cook lived a few miles from Carlton at **Great Ayton**. His cottage was dismantled brick by brick some years ago and rebuilt in Australia but his old schoolroom remains as a museum to his memory. On the moor east of Great Ayton is the Captain Cook Monument. Also nearby is the interesting market town of **Stokesley**.

towards the crags and swing right following the ridge. Continue to the junction with the causeway – the Cleveland Way. Stone for this Rolls Royce of a footpath was brought to the summit by helicopter. Turn left and pass the gliding club, proceeding to the summit on the left-hand path. Follow the stepped path down to the track just before the road.

❺ Turn left on the track and merge with the road, following it round the sharp left-hand bend. Go through the car parking area on the right-hand side of the road and merge with the footpath, cutting off the road's 90° bend. Go right at the road and through the gate by the cattle grid, continuing for 200 yards. Go left along the access to Carlton Bank Stud and cross the stile at the right-hand side of the gate. Walk on for 100 yards and turn right, dropping down between a hedge and a coppice to a stile. Cross a series of fields and stiles, keeping straight forward to a road. Turn right into Carlton and swing left by the wrought iron bench following the public footpath sign over a footbridge back to the parking area.

ULLESKELF

Length: 3½ miles

Getting there: From the A64 York-Leeds road, go south from Tadcaster on the A162 for 2 miles and turn left before entering the village of Towton on Raw Lane. Proceed for 2 miles to Ulleskelf. Rail transport is an option. Ulleskelf station is open and can be reached via either Leeds or York.

Parking: Park on-street in the village.

Map: OS Landranger – York (105) (GR 519399).

In every season, coils of mist snake from the river Wharfe and envelope Ulleskelf in an all pervading langour. The last barges to this once bustling Viking village were tied up years ago and save for the clatter from the nearby railway, all is peace and tranquillity. Ulleskelf was formerly a centre for osiery production, seven basket makers harvesting willow from the Wharfe ings. Today only one craftsman continues the art.

The river Wharfe has, from time immemorial, attracted sportsmen. The Norsemen hunted here, the wildfowling Prince of Wales visited the area in 1871 and in all seasons, modern anglers con-

FOOD and DRINK

The Ulleskelf Arms will sustain you with substantial fare such as gammon and eggs, roast chicken and steaks. It is open for evening meals but at lunchtimes on Saturdays and Sundays only. Telephone: 01937 832136. At Stutton, just south of Tadcaster, the personally recommended Hare and Hounds provides an extensive menu. Telephone: 01937 833164.

tinue the pursuit of dace, chub, barbel and flounders.

Architecturally, the village is undistinguished although the oddly oblong Old Ship Inn and the imposing Ulleskelf Arms are worthy of note. The latter building's 17 chimneys suggest a busy past.

Three and a half miles . . . along the restful banks of the river Wharfe, through the sleepy hamlet of Kirkby Wharfe and over yawning fields by an old hall . . . relaxation indeed!

THE WALK

❶ From Ings Road (in the centre of the village) walk north upstream and pass the Old Hall, swinging right past the village hall and St Saviours chapel. Swing right again past the post office and go left in front of the Ulleskelf Arms. Cross the road, then turn right up the hill and cross the railway bridge, continuing for 100 yards. Go sharp right on West End Approach and follow the cul-de-sac road round to the left. Keep heading straight forward at the next left-hand bend on a track and cross a bridge, going left to a stile.

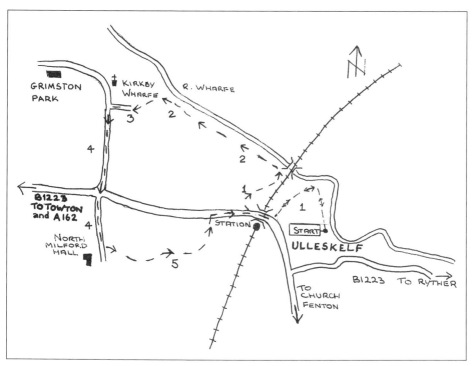

John Taylor, the last basket maker in Ulleskelf.

❷ Cross and head 30° right across a field to the corner. Cross a stile and keep hedgeside to a second stile. Go over this and continue to the river bank. (Until a few years ago, a chain operated ferry boat crossed from here.) Turn left upstream. Over a stile, keep going forward on the path. Ahead, the breweries of distant Tadcaster and, to the left, the tower of St John's church, Kirkby Wharfe, soon come into view.

❸ Just before the bend, drop down off the embankment to the corner of the field and go left 90° under the cables. Go left over a stile and immediately right over a second stile onto a track following a yellow arrow marker. Swing left by an orchard and turn right by the Jubilee Cottages, dated 1897.

❹ The route emerges near a broad triangular green. To the right is the back entrance gateway to Grimston Park (the main access is off the A162 – see 'Places of Interest') which was built in 1840 for Lord Howden and his wife, a Russian princess. Next to the gateway is the little church of St John (key available from the vicarage down the lane). Although much restored in 1860 it contains a wealth of antiquarian interest. A fragment of Roman marble by the vestry door bears an inscription to the daughter of an official. The tablet was found in a pigsty near the church. On the south wall of the chancel is a square relief, dated 1602, showing the kneeling figure of Thomas Leedes of North Milford Hall (which you will pass on the route).

❺ Swing left down the lane, passing the vicarage on the right and proceed, swinging slightly right to Raw Lane. Cross the road and go left, following the road signposted to North Milford. Walk on for 600 yards. To the right is North Milford Hall, an imposing 17th-century brick house of three bays.

❻ Turn left over a stile, following the public footpath sign for Ulleskelf. Continue for 300 yards and go left, using the ladder stile over a barbed wire fence onto the embankment. Turn right on a path, continuing to a gate. Go through, and swing right and then left down the edge of a field. Swing left at the field end and walk on to Raw Lane. Cross and turn right, using the footway back into Ulleskelf.

RIEVAULX

Length: 5½ miles

Getting there: From Helmsley on the A170 Scarborough-Thirsk road take the B1257 north-west for 4 miles to reach Rievaulx.	Parking: This walk begins with a visit to Rievaulx Abbey (fee payable). English Heritage have a small visitor centre and a car park in the village.	Maps: OS Landranger – Malton and Pickering (100) and Outdoor Leisure – North York Moors Western (26) (GR 575850).

The candles of the 12th-century Rievaulx Abbey have long been snuffed out but there is an ingraining spirituality in this Cistercian shrine by the Rye like few places in England. Led by St William, the French monks who came from Clairvaux in 1131, built well and by 1150 their great abbey was home to 140 monks and 600 lay brethren. And, excepting Fountains, there is more left standing at Rievaulx than at any other Cistercian abbey in the country. The ruins, in an incomparable woodland and river setting, are instantly balming, imaginings of coiling incense and the chants of cowled brothers hanging on the wind. The little

FOOD and DRINK

The great modern paradox in Rievaulx is that there is no inn. They closed it down 200 years ago! This would never have happened in St William's day. The English Heritage Centre offers tea and coffee. Close by is Helmsley, a busy market town offering a selection of cafés, restaurants and inns.

village of Rievaulx clusters round the abbey which provided stone for its cottages and mill.

The monks blessed this landscape and have left a legacy of unspoilt trackways and a history of monasticism that adds interest to every mile. A second band of brothers from Furness in Cumbria had originally intended to erect their abbey at Tylas Farm around 1145, but they transferred to the rebuilt Saxon church and village at Old Byland. The route visits both places and is so redolent of the old religious orders that it deserves to have its own name – I will christen it 'The Abbot's Trod'.

THE WALK

❶ After visiting the abbey, leave the parking area and turn right on the road. Go left, opposite the abbey, along the footpath marked to Bow Bridge. Go through five gates, walking fieldside to the river. Cross a stile near the river and veer right upstream for 100 yards. Turn right across the meadow to a stile. Cross and turn left on a track to the bridge.

❷ Cross the bridge and continue on the track for 120 yards before turning right, following a footpath sign over a stile towards Hawnby. Follow the yellow arrow

marker in the direction of the escarpment along the edge of the field and swing left to the stile. Walk alongside the Rye, entering the woodland. Drop down the steps onto the boardwalk and continue, leaving the wood and crossing a meadow. Swing left through bracken to a stile. Cross onto a road and continue to Tylas Farm.

❸ Opposite Tylas Farm, go sharp left up a track, climbing to a gate. Go through and walk left of the barn, continuing through a second gate and arcing left. At the top of the valley, go right over a stile, following the public footpath sign to Old Byland. Cross a stile in the field corner and follow a hedgeline left. Cross a second stile in the field corner, keeping fenceside. Cross a third stile and walk on, fieldside, to the next corner, then go 90° left, following the footpath sign to Old Byland. Go through the gate and keep hedgeside. Pass the barns and cross the stile in the field corner,

PLACES of INTEREST

Near the abbey is the half-mile long Rievaulx Terrace, in reality part of the lavish landscape gardening of Duncombe Park. Constructed in 1758, the terraces are jewelled with two temples, one having an ornate interior roof painting which took three years to complete. Nearby is **Duncombe Park**. It was originally built in 1713 and rebuilt in 1879. For 60 years it was used as a girls school until 1965 when it was taken back into family ownership and restored by Lord and Lady Feversham. It is open to the public, containing 'grand interiors', family portraits and collections of furniture. The 30 acre 18th-century garden, set in dramatic parkland has been described as 'the supreme masterpiece of the art of the landscape gardener.' A popular tourist centre, **Helmsley** is noted for its 12th-century castle and speciality shops.

All Saints church, Old Byland.

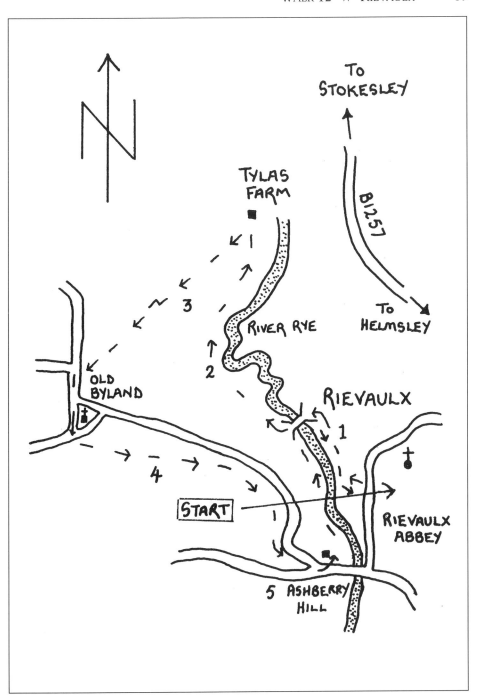

then turn right on the road. Turn left into Old Byland.

❹ Just left of the green is the church of All Saints. Around the porch are two carved Norman fragments, one showing dragons. On the east side of the porch (10 ft up) is a Saxon sundial.

Swing right going through the village and, opposite Southside, go left through the gate, following the public bridleway sign. Drop downhill left on a footpath and a heavily nettled track in the bottom of the narrow valley and go left of the pheasantry. Continue to the concrete track. Turn right for 10 yards and go immediately left, continuing forward in the valley bottom on a path. Cross over a stream with the meadow to the right and enter the woods, following the track as it gradually arcs left.

❺ Emerge on a road and turn right, swinging round to the left. At Ashberry Farm, turn left following the public footpath sign near the white barn. Go left of the farmyard through a gate, following a yellow arrow marker. Swing left uphill and follow the track as it drops down. Go through a gate and continue forward alongside a wood. Cross a stile by a gate and keep forward to the next gate. Go through and turn right on the track to the bridge over the Rye. Retrace your steps back to the village.

UPPER POPPLETON

Length: 9 miles

Getting there: From the A59 York-Harrogate road, turn due north on the signposted access road to Upper Poppleton,	3 miles north-west of York. **Parking:** Ample on-street parking is available around the	extensive village greens. **Map:** OS Landranger – York (105) (GR 555541).

Quiet and reflective, Upper Poppleton and its neighbour Nether Poppleton, are girded by a bend of Old Man Ouse, a rocking chair of a river, creaking, taciturn and slow. Immensely picturesque with an assembly of finely preserved cottages and farmhouses, the centre of Upper Poppleton is crowned by a fine maypole, stands of sovereign trees and a crop of splendid

chimney pots. Nearby is the church of All Saints built in 1898. A small nature reserve has been created in part of the unused churchyard. The magnetic attraction of both villages is the Ouse.

What better setting for a cinematic blockbuster about a certain mole! Packed with riverine and rural delights, this epic 9 mile ramble along the banks of the Ouse

---

FOOD and DRINK

Overlooking The Green, the Lord Collingwood inn offers freshly made and wholesome bar food. Alongside speciality stir fries and curries are more traditional English dishes such as gammon and Yorkshire puddings. Children are welcome for meals. This Mansfield house has an inviting beer garden in the shadow of the church tower. Telephone: 01904 794388.

---

and Nidd, enjoys long distant views and glimpses of two distinguished houses – Beningbrough Hall and Nun Monkton Priory. When our subterranean hero was faced with such a prospect he 'waggled his toes from sheer happiness, spread his chest, 'and said '"What a day I'm having! Let us start at once!"'

THE WALK

❶ From The Green, swing right on the road signposted to Knapton and York. Pass All Saints Hall and turn left on Long Ridge Lane. Turn next left down Dikelands Lane, continue and swing left to a T-junction opposite the school. Turn right along a signposted footpath that threads its way between houses to Nether Poppleton. This romantic old village reeks of antiquity, its fortunes having been inextricably entwined with those of nearby York. St Everilda's church was founded in 1130, part of its fabric coming, it is believed, from surplus materials left over from the building of York Minster. Close by, on Manor Farm, is a 500 year old tithe barn that has sheltered distinguished company. In 1644 Prince Rupert rested here before the battle of Marston Moor and in 1660 Lord Fairfax billeted 300 troops in the barn on the eve of proclaiming Charles II, king in York.

❷ Turn left on Main Street (the Lord Nelson inn is 100 yards on the right), pass a cottage named Saxe Dane and fork right, following the riverside footpath signposted 'Yorvik Way'. Continue, following the curving bank of the Ouse for about 3¼ miles to the confluence with the river Nidd. Both Nun Monkton Hall and Beningbrough Hall preside over the placid greeting of the waters, many river craft tying up to enjoy this sublimely peaceful spot. The privately owned Nun Monkton Hall, behind its topiaried boundaries over the Nidd on the left, was built in 1690 to classical designs. Across the Ouse on the right, Beningbrough Hall,which is open to the public, was completed, in an even more grander style, around 1716.

❸ Swing left along the bank of the Nidd and keep veering left going through a double gate and passing along a hedge to a caravan park access road. Turn right along the access road and cross a cattle grid to the edge of the village of Moor Monkton. Turn left, following the road signed as a public bridleway. Blue arrow markers designate the route from here on in.

❹ Keep going straight forward through a gate, walking under power lines. Continue through two further gates and at the fourth gate, veer left by a ditch towards a wood. Go through another gate and walk on alongside the edge of the trees for 150 yards, then turn sharp right and follow a thin hedgeline to the road.

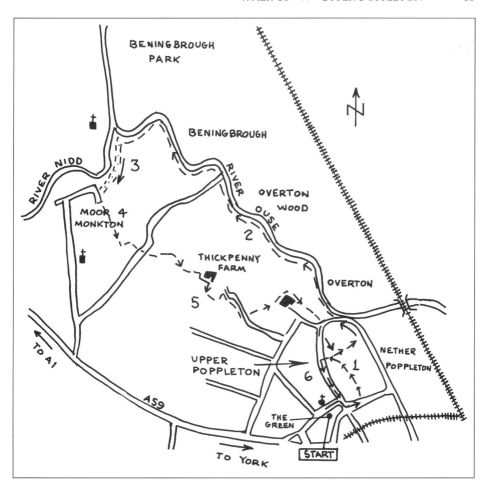

❺ Cross the road and continue along the Thickpenny Farm access road. Go through a blue gate and steer left and swing right by the bungalow and the farm buildings, negotiating two more gates. In the field corner, turn sharp right along the boundary and at the next corner, go through a gate and turn sharp left, going in front of the modern farmhouse along the field edge. Drop down, cross the dyke and a stile and continue uphill to the right of derelict farm buildings. Turn right opposite these on a track for 400 yards and go left, following a public footpath sign. Swing left by the dyke and arc right at the back of the farm, continuing through the farmyard – notice the old dovecote on the right. Keeping straight forward, walk on, fieldside, crossing a stile to the road and Upper Poppleton.

❻ Turn right and go left on Riversvale Drive for 200 yards. Turn right on the previously walked footpath to the school.

A self-closing gate!

PLACES of INTEREST

Beningbrough Hall: Circuitous access from Upper Poppleton is via the A59 and A19. Go south-east on the A59 for 1½ miles and then left on the Clifton road to the A19. Turn left and proceed for 4 miles to the outskirts of Shipton, leaving the A19 and proceeding left on a minor road to the hall. In addition to the Georgian splendour of the interiors which are decorated with over 100 portraits from the National Portrait Gallery, the hall offers beautiful flower borders, a walled garden and a Victorian potting shed. Open Saturday to Wednesday and Good Friday from 11 am to 5 pm, also Fridays in July and August. Telephone: 01904 470666.

Veer left on the road, passing the County Library and Chantry Green and turn right back to The Green and the starting point.

HOVINGHAM

Length: 7 miles

Getting there: For spectacular access with views of Castle Howard and its estate, go due north off the A64 at Barton Hill between York and Malton. Turn left along the B1257 in Slingsby, driving on into Hovingham.

Parking: Park around the village green.

Map: OS Landranger – Malton and Pickering (100) (GR 666758).

Picture book Hovingham is an unspoilt estate village encompassing the visions that make exiles pine for England. Its orderliness is that of the clipped yew, its attractiveness that of the embroidered feather bed, its pace that of the grandfather clock. With three greens, a stream, a church, an old hall shaded by lime trees and a circle of embowered cottages, together with a tea shop and a relaxing old inn, it is a place in which to linger.

On the old Roman road between Malton and Boroughbridge, Hovingham is of great antiquity. Fragments of a tessellated pavement, a bathhouse and hypocaust have been unearthed in the

---

FOOD and DRINK

The Hovingham Tea Rooms on Park Street (closed Christmas to Easter) serve home-made soups, flans, quiches and cakes – Yorkshire farmhouse teas are a speciality. Telephone: 01653 628881. The Malt Shovel Inn offers substantial lunch and evening bar meals (meat and poultry predominate). Telephone: 01653 628264.

---

area, which was once part of the ancient Forest of Galtres. Parts of this still survive, one tree, the King Oak being over 900 years old. All Saints' church was rebuilt in 1860 incorporating a unique sculptured Saxon stone and two beautiful 13th-century lancet windows. Hovingham Hall, built by Thomas Worsley in 1760 in the Italianate style, has many unusual features not least the impressive riding school entrance hall. The commodious Worsley Arms was erected in anticipation of the development of a spa. Springs, possessing 'powerful medicinal virtues', were discovered near the village around 1838 but despite the formation of a shareholders' company, the scheme came to nought. In later years the LNER railway ran near Hovingham. The route of the now abandoned line forms part of our walk.

Outward bound, the walk treads pleasant field paths and follows the track of the old puffers between Hovingham and Slingsby stations, only the width of the path and the occasional embankment clinker betraying the crime that was perpetrated here. Oh for the days of more civilised travel! In Slingsby the walk passes the spooky ruins of a 17th-century castle (built for a dwarf) before rising, by

way of delicious contrast, into woodland with long distance views.

THE WALK

❶ Walk down Park Street and turn right on Church Street, passing the magnificent entrance to Hovingham Hall on the left. Pass All Saints' and turn left past the Methodist church, crossing the little bridge over the stream on Brookside. Turn right and then right again, recrossing the stream over the footbridge near the Spa Garage, and go over the main road (B1257). Turn right, passing the Malt Shovel and, just beyond the car park wall, turn left following the public footpath sign.

❷ Walk alongside the tennis courts and bowling green, continuing straight forward hedgeside. At the end of the long field, cross the planked bridge and turn left along the next field edge for 150 yards

---

PLACES of INTEREST

Just 6 miles south-east of Hovingham is the internationally renowned **Castle Howard**. Designed by Vanbrugh, who had no architectural training and was the military and literary son of a baker, it was started at the turn of the 18th century. In baroque style, it is enormous and sublime, its size causing one contemporary commentator to suggest Vanbrugh was possessed by 'a passion for size amounting to megalomania', a characteristic satirised in the famous epithet: 'Lie heavy on him earth, for he laid many a load on thee.' The house and extensive gardens are open to the public. **Nunnington Hall**, 2 miles north of Hovingham, can also be visited. A 17th-century manor house, it contains a wealth of period pieces and has an interesting collection of miniature rooms.

Looking towards Hovingham.

before going 90° right, following the yellow arrow marker atop a post fieldside. In the field corner bear left and swing right through a gap in the fence still following the yellow arrow marker. Continue between two fields, veer right and proceed along a footpath and a farm track to a bungalow.

❸ Swing left and go right at the side of the bungalow on a marked public footpath along the dismantled railway track. At the road, cross the beck on the bridge and turn right into Slingsby. Pass the Grapes Inn (bar meals) and turn right along Church Lane passing the church and swinging left past the castle. Slingsby Castle was erected around 1620 for Sir Charles Cavendish, the brother of the Duke of Newcastle, a commander with the Royalist forces during the Civil War. Although a diminutive fellow, Cavendish was described as a man with 'a lovely and beautiful soul'. Oblong with four corner projections and a vaulted basement, the castle was abandoned after the battle of Marston Moor and forfeited to Parliament.

❹ Walk on uphill to the B1257 and cross. Turn right on the wide verge for 300 yards and go left, following the public footpath sign uphill, continuing to the wood. Enter the edge of the wood through a gate and turn immediately right for 80 yards, going left through the wood and following the yellow arrow marker for 400 yards. Turn right along a track and at the next inter-

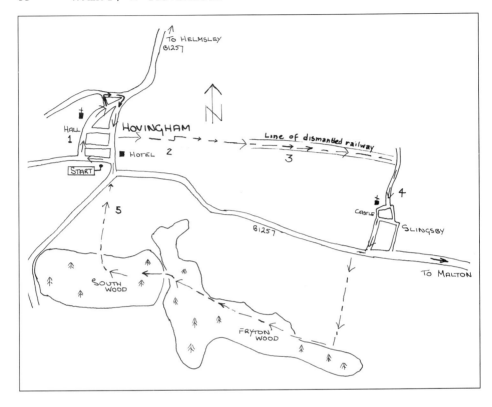

section, keep going straight forward following the public bridleway sign along the Centenary Way. Drop down, and, ignoring the right turn (blue arrow marker) keep going straight forward, swinging left downhill to a clearing (a splendid place for a picnic). Cross the meadow to the bridge and go over the stream, continuing right uphill through a gate into the woods and swinging left at the fork. Just past the woodman's shed, turn right on a woodland track and keep going forward following a blue arrow marker.

❺ Leave the wood and walk on a track between two fields, dropping down to the road. Turn right on the road and go left back into the village.

DUNNINGTON

Length: 6 miles

Getting there: Dunnington is due east of York and is easily accessible off the York bypass taking either the A166 or the A1079.	Parking: Park on York Street in the centre of the village.	Map: OS Landranger – York (105) (GR 668526).

A former agricultural village noted for the production of farming implements and for the cultivation of chicory, Dunnington is an ancient settlement located between two Roman roads. Largely a residential area these days, it still retains many of its now converted farm buildings, a fine stone cross and the church of St Nicholas, dating from Norman times. Near the eastern boundary of North Yorkshire, Dunnington is close to the Wolds and the pleasant countryside and Forestry Commission woodland nearby afford good opportunities for rambling on well defined paths.

A meandering fields and forests walk

FOOD and DRINK

The attractive Cross Keys inn at the end of York Street, opposite the stone cross, has a flourishing lunch and evening bar meals trade, half the bar being devoted to dining. Fish, which includes plaice, lemon sole and mussels is prominent alongside steak and chicken dishes. Telephone: 01904 488847. The fish and chip shop on York Street is recommended – open every lunchtime (except Monday) and evening. Passing this establishment I was unable to resist the nasal assault, remembering a snatch of a poem from my tramping hero Alfred J. Brown: 'Charm it with thy enchanting wand, Dip't in thy golden batter, Plunge it into thy magic pond, Serve it! I need no platter.'

to the banks of the river Derwent, this enjoyable, flat ramble over parts of the Minster Way has a surprise view.

THE WALK

❶ Walk down York Street towards the Cross Keys and turn right at the T-junction on Common Road. Continue on the footway on the left of the green and go left down Intake Lane. Pass the recreation area and playing fields on the right and proceed past the new housing development on the left. The road narrows and leads on into open countryside.

❷ Swing right at the bend and then swing left, going right into the Forestry

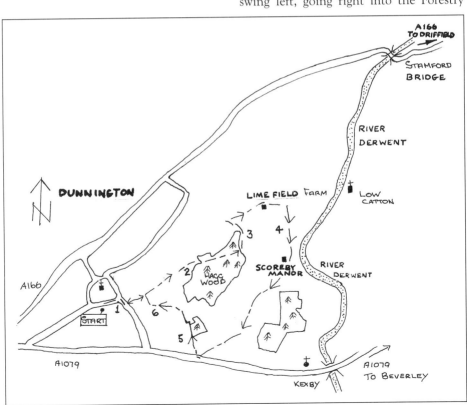

Commission's Hagg Wood through a gate. Walk on to a small clearing laid with chippings and go left on a pathway, continuing through tall pines. Keep going forward and exit the wood.

❸ The Plain of York ends abruptly to the east, the surprise view from the fringe of the wood taking in the undulating Wolds and the notorious Garrowby Hill to the north-east. Turn left along the perimeter of the wood and at the wood corner swing right, following the field edge. After 100 yards, turn right opposite the gate on a track which bisects a field heading towards Lime Field Farm. Swing right and go to the left of the farm, arcing right on a metalled access road from where the tower of Low Catton church across the Derwent comes into view.

❹ Where the road swings left, go right on the road, heading for Scoreby Manor House. Continue left and right, passing the house. Notice the date stone above the door, '1723' and the fire plaque. Turn left at the Londesborough Farm sign and swing right passing South Farm. Go right at the next bend, following the Minster Way sign and continue to the A1079.

❺ Turn right on the footway along this busy main road for 200 yards and then go right again following a public footpath sign over a bridged ditch and a stile. Keep hedgeside on a little used path to the edge of the wood. Follow the yellow arrow marker, keeping straight forward into the wood, and pass a cottage garden and a cottage to meet a track. Turn left on the track for 150 yards.

PLACES of INTEREST

Back along the A166, within little more than 5 minutes drive, is the **Yorkshire Museum of Farming** at Murton where many of the old farming implements made in Dunnington may be seen. The 8-acre grounds contain extensive displays, galleries and reconstructed interiors. South-east of Dunnington is the **Yorkshire Air Museum** at Elvington, housing the Barnes Wallace and Blackburn collections, a flight of vintage warplanes (Halifax, Mosquito, Hawker Hunter, Meteor, Buccaneer) a licensed NAAFI and a shop.

At this point the route deviates from that shown on the OS map, a local diversion order being in force.

❻ Turn right following the public footpath sign and arc round a tiny pond, continuing along the footpath between a hedge and a fence. At the 'Footpath Via Pond' sign, go left across the field towards the big tree (arrow marker on back of trunk) and walk 20° right across the next field. Veer diagonally across the final field towards the house and a white marker post and go left on the white track for 150 yards. At the field corner, turn right following the yellow arrow marker on a planked bridge over a ditch and go on past the allotments. Continue left to Intake Lane and proceed back into the village.

LASTINGHAM

Length: 4½ miles

Getting there: Lastingham is on the edge of the North York Moors National Park, north of the A170 between Helmsley and Pickering. Access through Hutton-le-Hole or Cropton.

Parking: Park on the lane up from the Blacksmith's Arms and the church.

Map: OS Landranger – Malton and Pickering (100) and Outdoor Leisure – North York Moors Western (26) (GR 728904).

Like a grouse hiding in the heather, Lastingham needs to be searched for. At the edge of the brooding Spaunton Moor and tucked in a hollow of the Hole Beck, the village seems to recoil from intrusive eyes and yet it is one of the most appealing in North Yorkshire. This holy place was chosen by St Cedd in the year AD 654 as a base for a monastery, the site being described by the Venerable Bede as 'more like a place for lurking robbers and wild beasts than habitations for man'. The original monastery which was probably destroyed by the Danes in the later half of the 9th century was re-founded in 1078 before being moved to York. What remains today is the 11th-century church of St Mary. It surmounts what is a true wonder of Christianity, an apsidal crypt dedicated to St Cedd. Pilgrims from all over the world come to this shrine to honour the saint and his real life brother St Chad who succeeded him as abbot.

In this holy place where the spirits of St Cedd and St Chad and their brethren are in the air you breathe, you too may find something that speaks to you of God.

The other prominent building in Lastingham is the Blacksmith's Arms, a fine 18th-century hostelry with a preserved Yorkshire range. The inn was once kept by a hard pressed curate's wife who had 13 children. Her husband, the Reverend Jeremiah Carter, was summoned before the church authorities for playing and dancing in the pub on the Sabbath. He answered his critics as follows: 'My wife keeps a public house, and as my parish is so wide that some of my parishioners have to come from ten to fifteen miles to church, you will readily allow that some refreshment before they return must occasionally be necessary, and when can they have it more properly than when their journey is half performed? Now, sir, from your general knowledge of the world, I make no doubt that you are well assured that the most general topics in conversation at public houses are politics and religion . . . To divert their attention from these foibles over their cups, I take down my violin, and play them a few tunes, which gives me

---

FOOD and DRINK

The Blacksmith's has a daily changing menu. Typical choices include locally-caught cod and haddock, celery and Stilton flan, bean and lentil lasagne, lamb casserole and pork steak in a cheese and mustard sauce. Telephone: 01751 417247.

---

an opportunity of seeing that they get no more liquor than necessary for refreshment; and if the young people propose to dance, I seldom answer in the negative; nevertheless, when I announce time for return, they are ever ready to obey my commands, and generally with the donation of sixpence they shake hands with my children, and bid God bless them. Thus my parishioners enjoy a triple advantage, being instructed, fed, and amused at the same time'. Amen. No more was said on the subject.

This gentle fields and hedgerows amble with peeps of the river Seven passes through a village which has a fascinating connection with the whaling industry.

THE WALK
❶ Walk east away from the church and, on the left, pass one of the three holy wells in the village. On the right, set into a building which was once the post office, notice the inscribed stone. It reads: 'The hap of a life Good or ill The choice of a wife.'

Swing right, round the bend and go left round the next bend. Continue for 100 yards and go right, following a public footpath sign through a gate. Swing right, fenceside, and cross a stile, then keep right to the next stile. Go left over the stile and

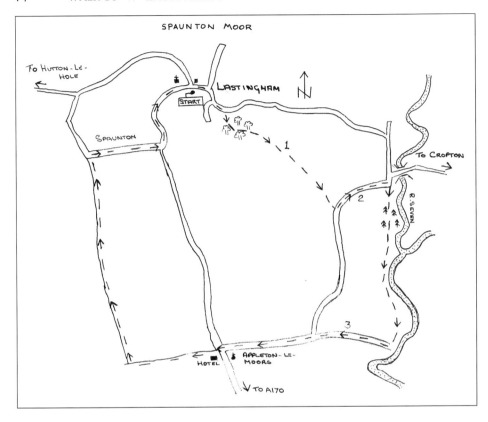

cross the stone bridge, swinging right on the track at the edge of a wood. Cross a stile and head for the top corner of a field, going through a gate and continuing fieldside to a stile. Cross onto a lane.

❷ Go left downhill and turn right just before the bridge, following a public footpath sign over a stile. Cross a stile and keep forward fenceside going through a gate at the end of the field into a wood. Follow the track – glimpses of the river Seven on the left – and gradually drop down to a field. Continue forward along the field and wood edge and merge with a farm track, continuing to a gate near a

farm. Go through and turn right on an ascending lane.

❸ Cross a cattle grid and continue along a lovely, leafy lane, swinging left into Appleton-le-Moors. The three most prominent buildings here – the church, the old schoolhouse and what is now the hotel – were built by Captain Joseph Shepherd. He ran away from home at the age of 12 and joined a whaling ship, returning many years later with a fortune which he bestowed on the village. The church was built in French Gothic style to a design by J. L. Pearson who was responsible for restoring Lastingham church and

Lastingham's former post office with its 'words of wisdom' above the door.

PLACES of INTEREST

The popular tourist haunt of Hutton-le-Hole, the home of the **Ryedale Folk Museum**, is 2 miles west of Lastingham. This prize winning attraction has 13 historic buildings showing 4,000 years of village life from pre-history to the 20th century. It is Yorkshire's leading open air museum. The buildings include an Elizabethan manor house with massive oak crucks and 18th and 19th-century thatched cottages. The museum also offers replica period shops and craft workshops, together with a wide range of farming and rural implements. It is open from March to October. Nearby is **Nunnington Hall**, a 17th-century manor house on the banks of the Rye. It has a magnificent oak panelled hall, cosy family rooms, and, in the attic, the amazing Carlisle Collection whose miniature rooms, each furnished to one-eighth life size, will delight any child. Also within easy reach is the village of Thornton-le-Dale. Its thatched cottages, roadside streams and rose-filled gardens have used up more rolls of film than Kodak.

for work on Truro cathedral. It is constructed mostly from the locally quarried Rosedale ironstone and houses a stirring array of windows. Turn right at the side of Appleton Hall Hotel along the signposted track and continue to the next signpost. Turn right, following the sign to Spaunton on a wide path between two fields. Leave the long field and swing right on a track, continuing to a gate. Go through and turn right into Spaunton. Go through the village and turn left, downhill back into Lastingham.

RUNSWICK BAY

Length: 7 miles

Getting there: Runswick Bay is off the A174 Whitby to Middlesbrough road.	**Parking:** A pay and display car park is available within yards of the beach, but beware the extremely steep descent.	**Maps:** OS Outdoor Leisure – North York Moors Eastern (27) and Landranger – Whitby (94) (GR 809159).

An impossibly pretty, rock-rose of a village rooted in the steep cliffside, Runswick Bay is every sailor's dream of a home from the sea. Organically grown with not a twopenny toss for planning regulations, its carefully painted, red-roofed cottages spill down to the beach, every nook and alleyway adorned with old anchors, figure heads, brasses, lanterns, tide-washed booty and hosts of bright summertime flowers. What a picture!

An old fishing and jet mining village, Runswick, apart from one solitary house, slipped into the sea in 1682. The loss was credited to bad luck and superstition has always been rife in these parts, fisherwives slaughtering cats to ensure heavy catches and the safe return of the fleet. Another

Port Mulgrave.

curious custom was performed in Hob Holes near the modern yacht station. Before the caverns were reduced by jet digging, mothers would take children with whooping cough to the spot, invoking the words:

'Hob – Hole Hob!
Ma bairn's getten t'kink-cough:
Tak't off – tak't off!'

With lungfuls of salt air spiced with hedgerow and woodland smells, this grand sweep of five contrasting villages is the cure for any ailment. The route heads inland to Ellerby, Newton Mulgrave and Hinderwell before returning on the clifftopped Cleveland Way past the enigmatic Port Mulgrave.

THE WALK
❶ Walk away from the village, south along the beach. If the tide is in, take the winding footpath through the scrub. Continue for about 600 yards and turn right by a wartime anti-tank block, going through a gate and heading away from the sea uphill through woodland. Go left at the concrete bulwark, climbing steeply on a muddy track and leave the wooded area, keeping forward between hedgerows. Go through the gate and swing left, crossing the line of the old railway. Follow the track left, continuing on Coverdale Lane. Continue for about 800 yards and turn right, before the bend, following a public footpath sign over a stile. Go forward, hedgeside, and swing right at the field corner, going through the gap in the hedge on a planked bridge. Cross a stile, heading right for the field corner. Cross a stile and keep forward, hedgeside, for two fields, crossing a stile to a road.

❷ Cross the road and walk into Ellerby turning right at the bend. Leave the village and just before the Ryeland Lane sign, turn left following a public footpath sign over a stile. Cross a field and stile, going left and right at the field corner. In the next corner, swing right and go left over a footbridge heading slightly right across a field towards a post (hidden in the first few yards). Cross a stile and go right, down a fenceline to the field corner. Go left for 100 yards and turn right through a gate, following the yellow arrow marker on a farm track. Cross the cattle grid, and turn left into Newton Mulgrave.

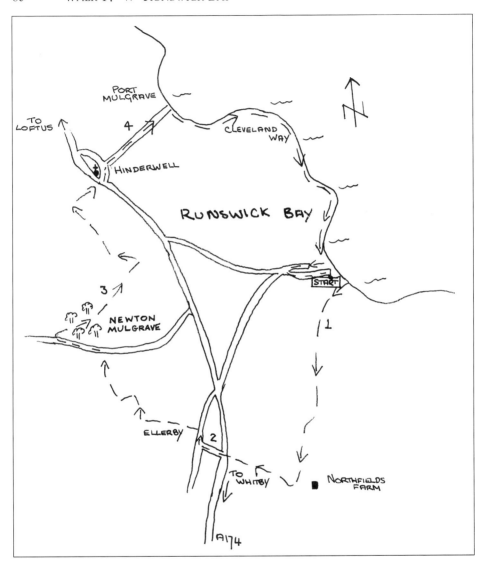

❸ Pass through the village, noting the inscribed stone on one of the cottages, 'Newton Mulgrave Town', and turn right following a public footpath sign over a stile. Arc right to the back of the farm and cross the stile, following the yellow arrow marker into a wood. Drop down right on a track and cross a footbridge in the bottom, ascending fenceside to a stile. Cross twin stiles and keep forward hedgeside to a stile. Cross and go left on a track – Back Lane. Continue to a T-junction of tracks and turn right into Hinderwell.

❹ Cross the A174 in Hinderwell and go left down the lane at the back of St Hilda's church. The saint is said to have rested here on her journey from Guisborough to Whitby Abbey and to have refreshed herself in the churchyard well which is still the focus of an annual well-dressing ceremony. Turn right on the road signposted to Port Mulgrave. Turn right at the end of the road, following the signposted Cleveland Way along the cliffs back into Runswick Bay. Before returning, you may care to explore Port Mulgrave.

A steep path leads down the cliffside to the crumbling, storm smashed jetties. An iron ore handling facility was built here by local man Charles Mark Palmer in the late 19th century. He lived at Grinkle Park north of Scaling reservoir. The ore was brought along a long tunnel (now blocked up at the seaward end) and transported on rails to the pier for shipment to the blast furnaces of Jarrow. The port is now the preserve of lobster fishermen and their wonderfully ramshackled sheds.

Runswick Bay.

WHARRAM PERCY

Length: 4 miles

Getting there: Wharram Percy is 6 miles south-east of Malton, off the B1248 road near Wharram-le-Street.

Parking: Park near the crossroads in Wharram-le-Street, down the Duggleby road near the post office.

Maps: OS Landranger – Malton and Pickering (100) and Scarborough and Bridlington (101), each showing part of the walk. (GR 865659).

As a village walk, the ramble to Wharram Percy is unique. The best known of some 40 such settlement sites in the Yorkshire Wolds, it is entirely deserted, the only surviving standing building being the ruined church of St Mary. The site has been extensively excavated, exhibits and details of village life being displayed in Malton Museum, a prior visit to which gives added interest to this already absorbing walk. For hundreds of years from the 11th century, Wharram Percy was a thriving agricultural community whose prosperity was based mainly on the rearing of sheep. What economic fortunes befell this place to cause mass migration and desertion?

Starting from the old Roman road in Wharram-le-Street, this scenic walk, with long distance views of the Wolds, strides the track of the abandoned Driffield to Malton railway line before visiting Wharram Percy. The path returns along a typical dry chalk valley. Geologically and topographically, this walk is firmly in the East Riding, but administratively, it is in North Yorkshire

THE WALK

❶ At the crossroads, take the road signposted to Birdsall and continue down the hill past the Wharram Quarry Nature Reserve. Swing right and go left on the old

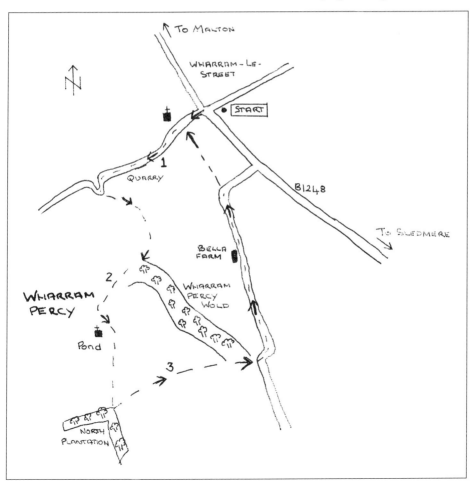

St Mary's church, Wharram-le-Street.

railway line, following the public footpath sign past Station Cottage. Continue to the bridge and go right, following the English Heritage sign to Wharram Percy through a gate.

❷ Swing left on the footpath. Some of the cottage sites are visible on the ground. Go left to the side of the old farmhouse. On the gable is the former Wharram station sign. It was removed from the trackside in 1940 at the time of the threatened German invasion and never reinstated. The line closed to passengers in 1950. Go through the kissing-gate towards the church . Part of it dates from the 11th century. One of its church bells now resides in the tower of St Mary's church in Wharram-le-Street. Go through the second kissing-gate following the yellow arrow marker to the left of the old fish pond – a fine spot for picnics.

❸ Go left over the stile, following the footpath sign to Thixendale. Climb to the top of the valley, going right along the ridge to meet the edge of the linear wood. Turn left, following the Wolds Way sign over a stile. Walk on past the wood, go through a gate and swing left on the quiet lane along the top of Wharram Percy Wold. Pass Bella Farm and at the bend, keep heading straight forward, following the Wolds Way sign on a path. In the field corner, go through a gap in the hedge over a stile and turn right, back to the starting point.

GOATHLAND

Length: 4 miles

Getting there: Goathland is west of the A169 Pickering to Whitby road.

Parking: Free parking is provided in the centre of the village, but because of

Yorkshire Television's Heartbeat connection (episodes are shot in Goathland) large numbers of tourists converge here during the summer months when space is at a premium.

Maps: OS Outdoor Leisure North York Moors – Eastern (27) and Landranger – Whitby (94) (GR 830011).

My first introduction to Goathland was through a haze of smoke and steam. Engine number 62765 Hunt Class 4-4-0 *The Goathland* was a regular visitor to my home shed of Neville Hill in Leeds, the Goliath conjuring up a vision of a far away Yorkshire village encircled by wild moors.

I eventually came to Goathland and was not disappointed, delighting in the discovery of its moorland howes and riggs and revelling in expeditions to the romantically named waterfalls of Mallyan Spout, Nelly Ayre Foss and Keld Scar Foss. Today, the free roaming sheep which once had

FOOD and DRINK

The Birch Hall inn in Beck Hole offers traditional fare such as pork pie and pickle, turkey and ham pie, roast beef and Yorkshire puddings and cream teas.Telephone: 01947 896245. Goathland's Mallyan Spout hotel is open for bar meals such as home-made soups, steaks, fresh Whitby fish and home-cooked ham. Telephone: 01947 896206. There is also a number of cafés in the village serving cakes and light snacks.

after the famous Goathland Hunt founded in 1750. It has one of the oldest packs in the country.

Following the route of an abandoned railway to the gem of Beck Hole, the walk accompanies the merry West Beck – a chortling, prancing *Riverdance* of a stream that at times will leave you breathless – before returning over moorland and fields. Occasional slippery boulders demand the wearing of stout footwear.

precedence on the village green have largely been displaced by tourists, but step just 100 yards beyond the main street and all is undisturbed. And, miraculously, the village is still served by steam railway on the North York Moors line from Pickering. My steam engine was, of course, named

THE WALK

❶ From the car park, turn left down Beckhole Road for 50 yards and go left through a kissing-gate, following a descending track to Beck Hole – signposted the Grosmont Rail Trail. The route follows the line of the old Whitby-Picker-

A familiar site to viewers of the hit TV series, Heartbeat.

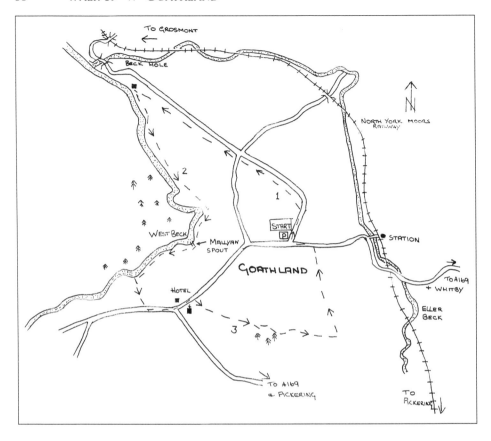

ing railway – the third to be built in the country. George Stevenson helped with the survey work. The track was so steep between Goathland and Beck Hole that coaches had to be hauled up the incline by a rope on a revolving drum, the load being counterbalanced by a four ton water tank which descended as the coaches were being pulled up. Charles Dickens rode 'this quaint old railway along part of which passengers are hauled by rope'. In 1864 a serious accident occurred as the rope snapped and several coaches went hurtling in the direction of Beck Hole. This prompted the engineers to divert the rail-

way onto its present route. Drop down, going through three kissing-gates to Incline Cottage at the bottom. The hamlet of Beck Hole, a few hundred yards off to the right, should not be missed. The Lilliputian bar of the Birch Hall inn is a sight to behold. I never knew two solitary customers could become so intimate. Experience it for yourselves.

❷ Just beyond Incline Cottage, turn left through the gate, following the yellow arrow marker along the banks of the West Beck. Follow the well defined path up and down, through a series of kissing-gates and over two footbridges and one board walk, continuing forward at the Mallyan Spout signboard. Pass this waterfall and keep going for about 450 yards. Leave the wood, crossing a wall over a stile and go left (no sign) weaving uphill on a track away from the beck. Veer left and continue uphill on a green path to the road. Turn left into Goathland. At the junction, go left into the village. Pass the church of St Mary and go right over the village green, following a public footpath sign through a gate.

❸ Cross a stile and follow the hedge, crossing a second stile and keeping fence-side. Swing left, dropping down to a footbridge. Cross and swing 180° left to a stile, crossing into the Abbot's House caravan park. Turn right through the park to a track and go left. Straight on, a few hundred yards down the lane, is Abbot's House, built near the site of a monastic cell established in the reign of Henry I by Osmund. Continue down the lane and go left into Goathland. Turn right on Beck-hole Road back to the car park.

PLACES of INTEREST

The steam journey to or from **Pickering** can add up to a memorable day. There are several exceptional inns in the town, which also has an interesting 12th-century castle and a church with some of the most important wall paintings in England – 'they give one a vivid idea of what ecclesiastical interiors were really like'. Dating from the mid 15th century, the paintings were only rediscovered in 1853 and were then whitewashed! A Yorkshire legend is to be found 5 miles south of Goathland on the A169. The fire of the **Saltersgate Inn** is said never to have been extinguished in nearly 200 years. An old smugglers' inn, it once served turf-cakes. The inn is an excellent starting point for a walking excursion along the Old Wife's Way to Blakey Topping.

BROMPTON

Length: 6 miles

Getting there: Brompton is 6 miles south-west of Scarborough on the A170.

Parking: Village parking is available behind the Cayley Arms inn.

Maps: OS Landranger – Scarborough (101) and Outdoor Leisure – North York Moors Eastern (27) (GR 945822).

Brompton-by-Sawdon, to give the village its full name, is an unassuming and retiring settlement beside a busy road to Scarborough. Apart from its roadside inn, it reveals few of its attractions to passing motorists, the majority of whom roar by, missing a halcyon scene that has inspired many a canvas and a history that changed the world.

Just a few yards back from the road is the lovely spired church of All Saints where the poet Wordsworth was married in 1802. The setting of this church which overlooks a pond graced by swans and ducks is indeed poetic, the springs percolating from the moors to the north feeding the Brompton Beck whose flow was impounded in years gone by to power the circles as the Father of Aerial Navigation, he is credited with building the world's first aeroplane, which was flown across Brompton Dale in 1852. His coachman test pilot successfully guided the craft over the 140 yard wide valley and promptly shouted: 'Please, Sir George, I wish to give notice. I was hired to drive, not fly.'

After enjoying the refreshing water margins, the route goes west along quiet farm roads to the village of Snainton before climbing steeply past Wydale Hall – Sir George's one-time home – to the head of Brompton Dale where the famous flight took place. There are stunning views all the way over the Derwent valley to the gently sloping Wolds in the east.

local mill. Today, the beck dances unimpeded through cool and immensely inviting emerald green water meadows.

Brompton has long been associated with the Cayley family, whose distinguished son George, the 6th baronet (1773–1857), ought to be as well known as Amy Johnson and Alcock and Brown. A prolific inventor, known in scientific

All Saints church and the pond.

THE WALK

❶ Go west from the car park and cross the road, continuing forward on Church Lane. Opposite All Saints' church, go left, following the public footpath sign through a kissing-gate and passing a pond. Go left through a second kissing-gate by a cottage and immediately right down the steps at the side of the cottage, following the road down. Turn right at the junction along the quiet road and swing left. Swing right and pass the caravan site. At the cross roads, turn right into the village of Snainton.

❷ Cross the A170 and keep straight forward uphill on the road. Continue going forward on the track and after about 600 yards, turn right, following a public foot-

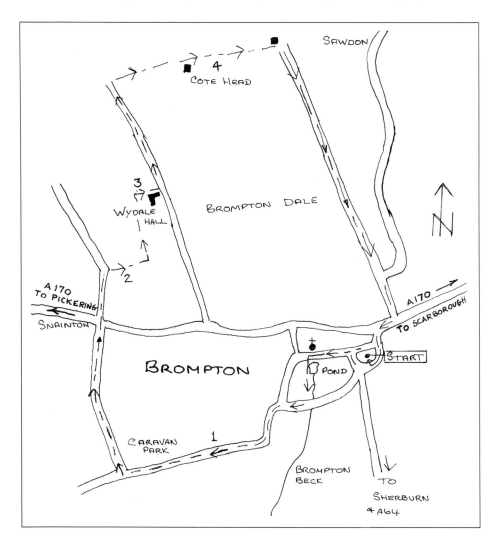

PLACES of INTEREST

About 200 yards west of the Cayley Arms along the main road is a fairly anonymous looking building bearing a small green plaque. It reads, in part, 'scientific aeronautical experiment was pioneered from this building – here the aeroplane was defined for the first time'. Some 4 miles north-east, just beyond East Ayton, is the **Honey Farm** with exhibitions of bees and bee products. The picturesque **Trouts Dale**, known as the 'Little Switzerland of the North' is 3 miles north of Snaiton.

path sign over a stile and keeping hedge-side. In the field corner go through a gate, following the arrow marker left and gradually descending on a path to the valley bottom, approaching Wydale Hall. This impressive building in a stunning location is now a retreat for the Diocese of York.

❸ In the bottom, go left over a stile following a yellow arrow marker near a massive fir tree and swinging right on a woodland track at the back of the hall. After 300 yards go right, following the yellow arrow marker into the wood, and keep going straight forward, passing alongside a five-a-side football pitch. Go through a kissing-gate left, following a yellow arrow marker along the concrete road. Go through another kissing-gate, then follow a yellow arrow marker right and at the road go left.

❹ Pass Headon Farm and as the metalled road gives out keep going forward on the tree-lined track. At the corner of the wood, turn right following a public bridle-way sign through a gate and keep wallside. To the right is the top of Brompton Dale. Go through a gate and swing right on the track, keeping right to the next gate. Go through and walk on, passing Cote Head. At the Cote Head Farm sign, turn right, down the descending track. Merge with the road and keep going forward on the verge to the A170. Cross and go right and left down Hungate for 200 yards. Turn right by Milford Cottage and fork right by the old mill on the footpath back to the car park.

Tourist Information Centres covering the area include:

Beverley – The Guildhall, Register
Square, Humberside HU17 9AU
(tel. 01482 867430)

Ilkley – Station Road, West Yorkshire
LS29 8HA
(tel. 01943 602319)

Boroughbridge – Fishergate,
North Yorkshire YO5 9AL
(tel. 01423 323373)

Ingleton – Community Centre Car Park,
North Yorkshire LA6 3HJ
(tel. 01524 241049)

Danby – The Moors Centre, Danby
Lodge, Lodge Lane, Whitby YO21 2NB
(tel. 01287 660654)

Knaresborough – 35 Market Place,
North Yorkshire HG5 8AL
(tel. 01423 866886)

Easingwold – Chapel Lane,
North Yorkshire YO6 3AE
(tel. 01347 821530)

Leyburn – Thornborough Hall,
North Yorkshire DL8 5AD
(tel. 01969 23069)

Grassington – National Park Centre,
Hebden Road, North Yorkshire BD23 5LB
(tel. 01756 752774

Northallerton – The Applegarth Car Park,
North Yorkshire DL7 8LZ
(tel. 01609 776864)

Great Ayton – High Green Car Park,
Great Ayton, Middlesbrough TS9 6BJ
(tel. 01642 722835)

Pateley Bridge – 14 High Street,
North Yorkshire HG3 5AW
(tel. 04123 711147)

Harrogate – Royal Baths Assembly
Rooms, Crescent Road HG1 2RR
(tel. 01423 525666)

Pickering – Eastgate Car Park,
North Yorkshire YO18 7DP
(tel. 01751 473791

Hawes – Dales Countryside Museum,
Station Yard, North Yorkshire DL8 3NT
(tel. 01969 667450)

Richmond – Friary Gardens,
Victoria Road, North Yorkshire DL10 4AJ
(tel. 01748 850252)

Helmsley – Town Hall, Market Place,
North Yorkshire YO6 5BL
(tel. 01439 770173)

Ripon – Minster Road, North Yorkshire
HG4 1LT
(tel. 01765 604625)

Horton-in-Ribblesdale – Pen-y-ghent
Cafe, Horton, Settle BD24 0HE
(tel. 01729 860333)

Scarborough – St Nicholas Cliff,
North Yorkshire YO11 2EP
(tel. 01723 373333)

Scotch Corner – Pavilion Service Area
A1, Nr Richmond, DL10 6PQ
(tel. 01325 377677)

Settle – Town Hall, Cheapside,
North Yorkshire BD24 9EJ
(tel. 01729 825192)

Skipton – The Old Town Hall,
9 Sheep Street, North Yorkshire
BD23 1JH
(tel. 01756 792809)

Sutton Bank – Sutton Bank Visitor
Centre, Nr Thirsk YO7 2EK
(tel. 01845 597426)

Thirsk – 14 Kirkgate, North Yorkshire
YO7 1PQ
(tel. 01845 522755)

Wetherby – Council Offices,
24 Westgate, West Yorkshire LS22 4NL
(tel. 01937 582706)

Whitby – Langborne Road,
North Yorkshire YO21 1YN
(tel. 01947 602674)

York – TIC Travel Office,
6 Rougier Street, YO2 1JA
(tel. 01904 620557)

York – De Grey Rooms, Exhibition
Square, YO1 2HB
(tel. 01904 621756)

York – York Railway Station,
Outer Concourse, YO2 2AY
(tel. 01904 643700)